DONALD MACPHERSON

GREAT GLEN
CANOE TRAIL

A COMPLETE GUIDE TO SCOTLAND'S FIRST FORMAL CANOE TRAIL

2ND EDITION

Important notice – disclaimer

Paddlesports, whether in a loch, river or sea environment, have their inherent risks as do all adventurous activities. This guidebook highlights some considerations to take into account when planning your own Canoe Trail.

While we have included a range of factors to consider; you will need to plan your own trail and within that ensure there is scope to be adaptable to prevailing winds, weather conditions and ever changing river hazards. This requires knowing your own abilities, then applying your own risk assessment to the conditions that you may encounter. The physical nature of the Great Glen and the varying environmental conditions within the coastal waters, inland lochs and rivers means that every day good judgement is required to decide whether to paddle or not.

The information within this book has been well researched; however neither the author, Scottish Canals nor Pesda Press can be held responsible for any decision of whether to paddle or not and any consequences arising from that decision.

Second Edition 2020
First published 2011

Published in Great Britain by Pesda Press
Tan y Coed Canol
Ceunant
Caernarfon
Gwynedd
LL55 4RN

ISBN: 978-1-906095-74-1

Printed and bound in Poland. www.lfbookservices.co.uk

Foreword

I am delighted to be able to report that the Great Glen Canoe Trail has been a success for many years now, and that it offers the paddler a superb experience, and one of the best through canoe routes in the world.

I first paddled the route in 1977 with a group of friends, and in white water racing kayaks – not the best for carrying camping gear! We just drove up from England, camped at Corpach on the former campsite, and set off in the morning with an OS map – and completed the route. Later I did a fast passage in a marathon kayak for a bet, and finally in the 90s paddled the Great Glen at leisure in an open canoe, returning often since to paddle sections while on holiday.

Years later, when working as a consultant, I was contracted by the then Forestry Commission Scotland to research the Great Glen route, as it was thought to be the most paddled bit of Scotland. I therefore, during 2007, spent many happy hours driving up and down the A82, looking for canoeists. Everyone I spoke to thought the route and scenery were fantastic, but that there was an obvious need for greater infrastructure. Local businesses, meanwhile, saw very few canoeists and had no idea of the huge tourism potential.

British Waterways Scotland (now Scottish Canals) then took up the challenge, and so the plan for the Canoe Trail, and the Great Glen Canoe Trail Partnership, and subsequent funding, developed. I was happy to be involved in helping to make this wonderful trail more accessible to paddlers, and the trail is now in the hands of Scottish Canals.

I welcome all of you most warmly to Scotland and the Great Glen, and hope you enjoy your paddling.

Eddie is a kayaker and canoeist with over 60 years' experience, having paddled all over both western and eastern Europe, the USA and Canada and southern Africa. He is a former Board Director and Chairman of the Scottish Canoe Association.

© Photo | Polly Pullar

Contents

Sea Kayaks on Dores beach. Photo \ Donald Macpherson

The Author

Having been born and brought up in Inverness, the Highland Capital, I have regularly travelled the Great Glen by boat, by boot and by bike. Being offered the opportunity to develop and promote what I now refer to as 'my back garden' has been a fantastic opportunity because I was already established in the local outdoor industry with my own paddlesport business Explore Highland, and as a freelance instructor for a number of local paddlesports providers.

The post of Project Officer for the Great Glen Canoe Trail was always going to be exciting and challenging, while working with five publicly-funded organisations has itself been interesting! The two-year post from 2010–2012 included everything from negotiating with local landowners and passing on key information to the canal's lock keepers as well as supervising contractors' work. It was non-stop and although my two years passed very quickly I have made many friends and hopefully left a long-lasting legacy for all paddlers when they visit the Great Glen.

I do hope that my work and knowledge of the Great Glen, as demonstrated in this 2nd edition and online at www.greatglencanoetrail.info will help you to plan a safe journey through the Great Glen. It is a privilege to promote the Scottish Highlands as a fantastic paddling destination. Stay safe, respect and enjoy the trail!

Donald Macpherson

EXPLORE HIGHLAND - OWNER
SCA GREAT GLEN, RIVER OICH & RIVER NESS ADVISOR

Acknowledgements

A big thank you to everyone who has helped in compiling both the first edition and this second edition of the guidebook.

Thanks are also due to all those who have donated their time to help with the original photo shoot back in September 2010, and all my clients who have joined my many adventures since across the Great Glen and allowed me to use their photos in this second edition.

All photos are credited to the photographer within the captions in this second edition.

Using this Trail Guide

The Great Glen Canoe Trail is a fantastic 96km (60 miles) coast-to-coast journey that takes you through the very heart of the Scottish Highlands. Usually starting off in the west (Fort William) the Canoe Trail follows the Caledonian Canal eastwards to Inverness. With the current explosion in the popularity of paddle sports and the fantastic scenery and wildlife to be explored, it's no wonder over 4,000 paddlers a year are taking to this Canoe Trail. Though you may not be alone on the trail, you'll find plenty of space to experience that wilderness feeling when taking to the lochs.

With a choice of paddling the canal sections or running the Rivers Oich, Ness and Lochy, the Canoe Trail has plenty to offer paddlers of all abilities.

Although weather conditions can sometimes be very challenging, with proper planning, good local information and a safe, sensible approach to paddling, the Canoe Trail can be completed over three to five days. Some may plan longer to allow for taking their time and enjoying more of the local area and sights.

This book can be used in various ways. If you're experienced in multi-day paddling journeys, expeditions and being in the great outdoors, you may prefer to skip through some of the general sections and use the journey description to plan your route. Others with less experience may prefer to work through the 'Planning your Canoe Trail' section before moving on to the journey itself.

This book links in with the Great Glen Canoe Trail website which gives local resources and contact information, listing local canoe outfitters and services providers.

www.greatglencanoetrail.info

Another useful and up-to-date resource is:

www.explorehighland.com/great-glen-canoe-trail-map/

Trip grading

In order to give you some idea of the type of trip and conditions you might experience the trips are graded from A (easiest) to C (most difficult), based on the Scottish Canoe Association's open water trip grading. If you are a newcomer to paddling you should start off on a grade A trip so that you can judge your capabilities against other paddlers and minimise the risk to yourself.

- Grade A is in sheltered water. Participants should be capable of paddling 20km (12 miles) per day in Force 2/3 conditions.
- Grade B is in more challenging waters and may include tidal streams, exposed headlands, and open crossings between islands. Participants should be capable of paddling 25km (16 miles) per day in up to Force 4 conditions.
- Grade C participants should be capable of paddling in more difficult conditions than grade B for a longer time.

River grading

For the options that involve paddling on rivers the international river grading system is used. A river that can be grade 2 or 3 depending on water levels would be indicated with 2/3. Where a river is grade 1 but has short sections of grade 2 that could be avoided by portaging, this would be shown by using brackets, e.g. 1 (2).

- Grade 1, Easy. Occasional small rapids or riffles, waves regular and low. Most appropriate course, with deepest water, easy to see from canoe or kayak and steer down. Obstacles, e.g. pebble banks, very easy to see. Presents no problems to paddlers able to steer canoes and kayaks. Steering is needed, especially on narrow rivers.
- Grade 2, Medium. Fairly frequent rapids, usually with regular waves, easy eddies, and small whirlpools and boils. Course generally easy to recognise, but may meander around gravel banks and trees, etc. Paddlers in kayaks may get wet, those in open canoes much less so.
- Grade 3, Difficult. Rapids numerous, and can be continuous. Course more difficult to see, landing to inspect may be wise. Drops may be high enough not to see water below, with high and irregular waves, broken water, eddies and whirlpools/boils.

There are no waters with rapids of above grade 3 advised in this guide. Where there are grade 3 rapids, avoiding or portaging is possible.

How do you like to get afloat?

OPEN CANOE?

SEA KAYAK?

TOURING KAYAK?

PADDLEBOARD?

Experience?

What is your group like? Would you like to relax or be challenged?

No. of paddlers?

GUIDED TRIP

SELF GUIDED

Do you have your own boats?

Find a suitable Canoe Trail guide

NO

YES

www.**GREATGLENCANOETRAIL**.info

Number of days?

Choose between a planned guided trip or a bespoke trip?

Hire boats from a local Canoe Trail outfitter

Plan transport & shuttle

Route distance?

Plan your food

Your guide can arrange boats, kit, route, accommodation, food, shuttle & your canoe registration

Plan your camps & book accommodation

Apply for your canoe registration

ENJOY THE TRAIL

Planning your Canoe Trail

There are a number of factors that will help make your Great Glen Canoe Trail visit memorable – in a good way! Thorough planning, good kit, wholesome food, choosing your paddle team and a good night's rest each night can make all the difference to your adventure. Let's start with the basics – planning your adventure.

Making a plan

When planning your Canoe Trail visit you need to start thinking about the logistics of your expedition well in advance. Asking yourself some simple questions will help steer you to the right approach for you and/or your group.

Choosing your craft

One of the first decisions to make is which type of craft to choose. The four main types of craft that are recommended to take onto the Canoe Trail are open canoes, sea kayaks, touring paddleboards, and touring kayaks. Open canoes, sea kayaks, and touring paddleboards, are very well suited to expedition use. You can also use touring kayaks for day trips but as they have less storage space,

they can only hold limited supplies and food. However with good forward planning, topping up on your supplies throughout the trail and travelling light, they could be used successfully for multi-day paddles.

Some groups paddle the trail using single and double sit-on-tops as well as inflatable kayaks. The majority of these recreational craft are not designed for multi-day journeying, or for bad weather and are generally not suited to the open-water conditions that can be regularly found on Loch Lochy and Loch Ness.

Guided or self-guided

Whether you want to take to the water independently, join a guided trip, or form your own group will depend on your skills, confidence

📷 *Discussing the day's paddle ahead from Corpach Locks. Photo | John Macpherson Photography*

and what you're looking for in your Canoe Trail adventure.

Being part of a planned Canoe Trail group, run by a local commercial provider, puts you in the care of a suitably qualified guide who knows the Great Glen and the changeable local conditions. If you needed to evacuate the trail because of unforeseen weather/ circumstances, your guide would also be able to help and make emergency shuttle arrangements. All craft, paddling and camping gear, and shuttle service are usually provided, leaving you free to look forward to and enjoy your trail even more.

Group size and skills

The next choice to make is how many people you will paddle with. Safety in numbers is always best. It is not advisable to paddle the trail alone. Some people do paddle the trail as a pair in a double kayak or canoe. However, if a single craft gets into difficulty in the middle of a rough loch, self-rescue is much harder and requires a greater level of knowledge and skill.

Capsizing can happen at any time, especially in choppy water conditions. We always recommend that people travel in groups on the Caledonian Canal so that there are plenty of other people around to assist in the rescue of paddlers in the water, craft and kit. Do remember that the speed of paddling and portaging does slow down should the group be too large. To comply with the Scottish Outdoor Access Code and be able to wild camp on the side of the lochs, groups should be small and I strongly suggest this number should be no more than ten paddlers.

Loch Lochy and Loch Ness are both classed as open water and are covered by HM Coastguard due to their vast size. Loch Ness is 37km (23 miles long) and over a mile wide in places. Due to the sheer volume of water, the cold water temperature only increases by a few degrees over the summer months, meaning any paddler who capsizes does not have long before cold-water immersion problems set in.

Safety and rescue skills in deep and choppy waters are essential. Under the British Canoeing scheme a Canoe Leader, Sea Kayak Leader (equivalent to old 4* qualification) would be the minimum qualification to lead a group of experienced paddlers in these conditions. For stand up paddleboard groups a similar qualification to the forthcoming British Canoeing Stand Up Paddleboard Inland Open Water Leader would be recommended.

When to take to the trail

Scotland's weather can be, to say the least, unpredictable. To best appreciate the full coast-to-coast route, the majority of paddlers take to the trail from late March to late September.

If you do want to paddle the trail during the winter months, please remember that the canal sections are prone to freezing over and sub-zero overnight air temperatures make it an unsuitable time for wild camping. Loch Oich regularly freezes over in the winter months, but the other three lochs are still suitable for idyllic day paddles, as long as you've got appropriate paddling gear and enough layers on.

Days on the trail

The type of craft you decide to use on the trail will make a huge difference to how long your journey will take. Paddleboards and canoes are generally slower than sea kayaks and travel at approximately 3–5 kph. Sea kayaks are designed to cut through the water more efficiently and travel at around 5–7 kph. It is easier to maintain these types of speeds over a day when you're travelling in smaller groups and in tandem crafts; larger groups of less experienced paddlers may well require more frequent rests so should allow themselves longer.

Make sure you give yourself time to explore the shoreline and enjoy the experience of being in the Scottish Highlands. When planning your schedule, remember to include time for comfort breaks, bad weather days, food stops and exploring the local areas. If you're travelling with children, it's especially important to include time for lots of stops along the way.

Weather

The main weather condition that paddlers should be wary of in the Great Glen is the wind. The prevailing south-westerly wind can funnel straight up the glen and seriously affect paddling conditions. A gentle tail wind can help you along and even give you the chance for some sailing to help you cross the lochs, but strong tail winds can create short, dumping waves that can cause problems for paddlers. (Waves of more than 3 metres in height have been recorded on Loch Ness.)

A light breeze or passing tour boat can cause waves large enough to cause a capsize. Photo | John Macpherson Photography

If you're not an experienced paddler, even light winds can capsize a kayak or swamp a canoe. This is one good reason why paddlers should stay close to the loch shorelines, to enable a quick exit or for shelter. To be as safe as you can be on the water, always check local weather reports during planning and be prepared to change plan according to conditions. Remember that a light tail breeze not only helps you cover more distance, it also keeps the infamous midge away!

Accommodation

Being self-sufficient on the trail is all part of traditional paddling expeditions – living off the land/water and being at one with nature really can make your adventure a more memorable and rewarding experience.

Whether you want to 'rough it' by wild camping or would prefer a bit of luxury after a day on the trail, the Great Glen has accommodation options to suit.

Informal camp areas

The Caledonian Canal is a Scheduled Ancient Monument, protected by Scottish Government legislation. This means that the land is managed and maintained by Scottish Canals and wild camping is not permitted on the canal banks. The canal staff have, however, designated specific areas along the route where small groups are allowed to camp. These are generally located near suitable toilet facilities. There are restrictions at informal camp areas, including limits on the number of campers permitted for a maximum of one night stay and whether fires are allowed. Each site has its own requirements. Paddlers cannot book and are not guaranteed space at these areas, so you will have to move on if maximum num-

Setting up camp at an informal camp area. Photo | Donald Macpherson

bers are reached. It is always best to set up camp early, giving you time to find a suitable alternative for the night if your initial planned site is occupied.

Access to toilet blocks and facilities is controlled through Scottish Canals. When you register for the trail, you can hire a facilities key to use along the way (while large groups are not allowed to camp in the informal campsites, they can use the toilets). More information is available on Informal Camp Areas at www.greatglencanoetrail.info and you'll also find out more on the information panels at each site.

Trailblazer Rests

The Great Glen Canoe Trail project has worked with a number of local landowners to create informal campsites along the Canoe Trail. Called 'Trailblazer Rests', these basic sites are designed to blend into their natural settings. Facilities at some of these sites may include composting toilet(s), a clear area to pitch tents, fire pits, log seating, boat racks and even three-sided shelters. Each site will be slightly different due to the local environment. Each Trailblazer Rest has its own information panel highlighting site guidance and local information.

Providing toilets at these key locations will help reduce the long-term damage and pollution to our fantastic countryside created by the 4,000 paddlers that are currently taking to the Canoe Trail each year.

As with the informal campsites, paddlers are not guaranteed space at the Trailblazer Rest sites and will have to move on if there are too many people already there. Some of the Trailblazer Rests are also available to walkers and cyclists following the other

Great Glen Way routes (but they are not suitable for large groups of over 10 people). You can find out more on Trailblazer Rest Sites on the on-site panels and at www.greatglencanoetrail.info.

Wild camping

Under the Scottish Outdoor Access Code (SOAC), wild camping is allowed in Scotland; however, wild campers must stick to the guidelines laid out in the code. Wild camping should only be done in small groups and for a short stay in any one place. For more on wild camping see page 71 or have a look at www.outdooraccess-scotland.com

Commercial campsites

There are a number of commercially operated campsites with good facilities in the

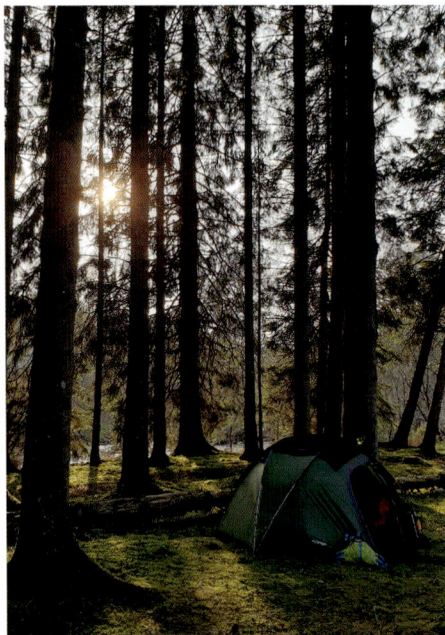
📷 Pitching a tent for the night in woodland.
Photo | Donald Macpherson

Great Glen. These sites are licensed by the local council and offer a variety of facilities including toilets, showers, wash areas and some even have drying areas for kit. You can find details of commercial campsites at www.greatglencanoetrail.info

Bunkhouses/B&Bs/hotels

The Great Glen is a very popular visitor destination so if you don't want to camp it out (or just not every night), you don't have to go far from the trail to find good places to stay ranging from basic bunkhouses to five-star accommodation. (Visit www.greatglencanoetrail.info where a list of accommodation can be found.)

You may prefer to mix your accommodation by combining camping with local guest houses to get that wilderness feeling, interspersed with the occasional night in a bed.

During the summer season it is always best to plan ahead and pre-book your accommodation. You may also find that you want to change your plans due to weather conditions. You're always assured of warm hospitality in the Highlands, and even if somewhere is fully booked, accommodation providers will usually do their best to help you find somewhere to stay in the local area.

Food planning

When thinking about food for the trail, the first thing to consider is what you shouldn't bring. Please avoid taking glass jars, bottles or fragile containers. These are easily broken during the journey so it's always best to transfer contents into a plastic container.

Due to the amount of extra energy you'll be using when paddling, portaging, setting up camp and living in the great outdoors you'll need to eat a lot more high energy foods. So, what are the best foods for energy on the trail? Dried foods such as cereals, rice and pasta are all great as they travel well, are high in calories and are excellent sources of carbohydrates. The shelf (or canoe) life of things like dairy products, fresh meats, fruits and vegetables is going to be shortened depending on what kind of storage you've got and the air temperatures. Rather than trying to carry lots of fresh food with you, a better idea is to pick up supplies as needed at Fort Augustus, the halfway point of the trail.

The Highlands of Scotland are well known for local produce, and it makes sense not to have to carry all your food for the whole journey from the start. In the Great Glen there are plenty food shops in Fort William, Fort Augustus & Inverness. There are also a number of smaller shops and cafés along the trail but may require a little walk to access them.

To help reduce group equipment and supplies, it helps to have a group menu and cook in bulk. This reduces the amount of stoves and pans needed and makes the group work better together off the water too. It requires a bit of forward planning and you should consider all group members' tastes and requirements when putting together your menus. Ensure that all group members are aware of any allergies other members of the group may have, especially if anyone suffers extreme reactions such as anaphylactic shock.

Remember, when out paddling you will burn calories and perspire a lot more through increased physical exertion. It is vital to ensure all paddlers are properly hydrated and that

Landing at the Well of Seven Heads to sample their cake and coffee. Photo | Donald Macpherson

everyone has enough fluids at hand to sip throughout the day.

Some buoyancy aids have handy built in water carriers in the back panel. These are really useful throughout the day and can hold between 1 – 1.5 litres.

Getting to the trail

Flights from London to Glasgow or Inverness make it much easier to get to the Great Glen from the south. Public transport to either Fort William or Inverness can easily be arranged through regular bus or train services.

Depending on your choice of craft and route you may have to organise a shuttle to ensure you have appropriate transport awaiting you at the end of your Canoe Trail. Joining a guided trip run by a commercial provider will take this part of the planning process off your hands as your provider will normally take care of this for you.

If you are travelling independently but hiring your canoes or kayaks, your canoe outfitter will also be able to offer you advice on recommended ways to complete the journey. One of the easiest ways to organise your trail is to meet your canoe outfitter at your finish point, where they can then shuttle you and your kit back to the start of the Canoe Trail. This makes for an easier finish to your trail as you've already done the shuttle and are ready to carry straight on with your onward journey. For those who are using their own craft and kit, some local canoe outfitters can also provide a simple shuttle-only service. Other groups using their own gear may opt to nominate one or two people to drop off their own craft at the start of the trail and then drive back to leave the vehicle(s) at the finish point. While their fellow paddlers pack and load the craft, the drivers can then take public transport back to the start point to rejoin the group.

Citylink and a number of service providers offer a regular bus service between Inverness and Fort William throughout the week (there is no train link). The bus journey takes about two hours, making a five-hour round trip.

Replenishing energy with Haggis, neeps and tatties.
Photo | John Macpherson Photography

A local bus service runs parallel to the trail.
Photo | John Macpherson Photography

Canoe registration

The Caledonian Canal today is still a working, living waterway and is managed and cared for by Scottish Canals. The majority of the waterways traffic passes through the canal from late March to early October. Outwith that time restricted services are offered when essential canal and lock gate maintenance is not being undertaken.

By registering your planned journey with the canals team, they can coordinate and manage the waterways safely and with nearly 50,000 boat movements (boats moving through lock gates and bridges) and 4,000 paddlers using the canal each year, registering your trail will also make your trip a lot safer and more pleasurable.

The registration process also acts as a simple check that paddlers and guides are aware of the types of waters and traffic that they will be paddling amongst – you'd be surprised how many aren't!

It is also a final opportunity to give useful safety and operational advice including other useful resources to help make planning your Canoe Trail easier. Collecting data on the number of paddlers using the Great Glen Canoe Trail enables the partner organisations to monitor its success and to apply for further funding to maintain and upgrade the facilities on the route for paddlers.

The Caledonian Canal office asks all paddlers to register at least 7 days in advance of your visit to allow them time to process your registration. The process is simple and can be completed online at www.greatglencanoetrail.info

Through the Scottish Outdoor Access Code, access to the Caledonian Canal is free to paddlers; however there may be a small charge for use of facilities such as toilets and showers which supports maintenance and upkeep. The canoe registration does not however include permission for paddlers to transit through the lock gate system (see page 29 on lining through locks).

📷 *Friendly lock keeper at work on the canal.*
Photo | John Macpherson Photography

📷 *Canoeists celebrate reaching the halfway point.*
Photo | John Macpherson Photography

Heavy Traffic on the Canal

Amongst the many and varied motor boats, yachts and freight vessels that use this busy waterway there are a number of regular, large vessels that include:

The **Jacobite Queen** along with the **Jacobite Rebel, Jacobite Maverick** and the **Jacobite Warrior** offer their award winning cruises, tours and charters from Dochgarroch Locks out onto Loch Ness to Urquhart Castle. At 23m in length and a beam of 5.5m, she may not be the biggest boat within the canal, but certainly one to look out for with her distinctive bow wake. www.jacobite.co.uk

Fingal and Ros Crana are holiday barges run by Caledonian Discovery Ltd, which operates the full distance of the canal offering walking, sailing and now paddling holidays. In fair weather they can also be seen out in Loch Linnhe and the Moray Firth. These converted barges have the capacity to accommodate 12 people living and sleeping aboard. As they are 39m long, manoeuvrability is always difficult so please give them space. https://www.caledonian-discovery.co.uk/

MV Lord of the Glens is a luxury cruise ship at just under 50 metres in length that when bought, back in the year 2000, was converted by a Spanish ship yard to have her beam reduced to 10.5m (maximum beam for the canal lock gates), allowing her to navigate from Inverness through the canal out to the Western Isles. www.lordoftheglens.co.uk

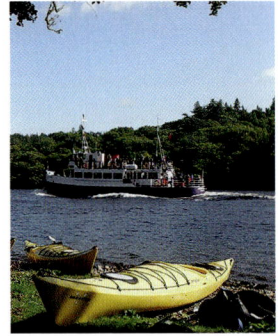

The Jacobite Queen producing wash on Loch Dochfour. Photo | Donald Macpherson

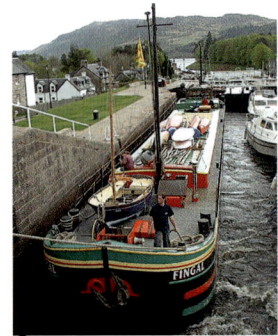

Fingal.
Photo | John Macpherson Photography

MV Lord of the Glens.
Photo | John Macpherson Photography

Equipment

It should go without saying that it's vital to take the right equipment with you when out on the Canoe Trail. We can all forget things so it's a good idea to write down a list of everything you'll need. To help you plan we have included a suggested kit list:

Personal Equipment

- Buoyancy aid
- Paddling clothing and footwear
- Camp clothes & shoes
- Sleeping bag & mat
- Hat(s) & midge net
- Toiletries, Towel
- Medication
- Head torch (wind up)
- Plate, bowl, cutlery & cup
- Water bottle & flask

Safety Equipment

- Emergency contact list
- First aid kit
- Whistle (worn on buoyancy aid)
- Survival bag
- Group shelter
- Mobile phone (in waterproof pouch)
- Repair kit
- Lock knife
- Spare torch & glow sticks
- Radio (wind up) for weather reports

Canoe Specific Equipment

- Spare paddle per canoe
- Canoe pole and sail
- Bailer & sponge
- Knee pads or kneeling mat
- Day bag
- Portage trolley per canoe
- Pump for portage trolley tyres per group
- Dry bag or barrel for packing gear into
- Small barrels for food/cooking stuff

River Paddling

- Helmet
- Throw bag & knife
- Slings & pulleys

Shared Equipment

- Tent(s) (small footprint 2 man is ideal)
- Stove/fuel
- Matches/lighter
- Toilet supplies
- Maps, compass & waterproof case
- Cooking set & utensils
- Food & water carrier
- Sunscreen & midge spray
- Spare rubbish bags

Optional Extras

- Waterproof camera
- Waterproof GPS
- Binoculars
- Tarp
- Kelly kettle
- VHF Radio
- Selection of flares
- Padlock to secure your boat
- Paddling mitts (pogies)

Sea/Touring Kayak Equipment

- Spray deck and paddle
- Split paddle (spare)
- Pump & sponge
- Towline(s)
- Kayak portage trolley or portage straps
- Small dry bags for packing gear into

Paddleboarding Equipment

- Pump, hose & connector
- Repair kit with suitable patches & glue
- Spare leash, fin & fin screws
- Ground anchor to secure over night

Loading your craft

Once you've got your gear together it is time to load your craft. Everyone has their own method developed over years of experience but if you're just starting out here are some top tips to help you! Space is at a premium so personal items should be kept to a minimum. Think carefully about what you may need and what you can do without.

When canoeing the Great Glen, all your personal items including your clothes, sleeping bag, your part of the tent, and mat should be able to fit inside a 60 litre canoe barrel or large dry bag. Fitting two paddlers, two barrels/large dry bags, portage trolley, food, cooking equipment and a day bag into your canoe means you have to be smart about what you take and how you load your canoe.

Dry bags or barrels? There are benefits to both. Using large rucksack dry bags rather than a barrel mean that you can carry your rucksack while pulling your canoe when portaging around the lock gates. If you take time out to hike up a Munro or have a short walk to a local accommodation provider, a rucksack dry bag is also a much better option.

Canoe barrels, however, do trap more air in them and if you capsize they offer greater floatation to you and your canoe (if attached properly). They also make excellent camp seats!

Think about how you are loading your boat and where you are placing the weight. Heavier bags should be placed in the centre to help balance and trim your canoe. You also need to think about what you might want to access quickly, for example, safety and rescue equipment must be easy to grab in an emergency. Small pieces of kit can be placed in your buoyancy aid pockets or within easy reach when afloat.

Next comes the food and cooking equipment. These items can be shared between members of the group to ensure that weight is evenly distributed across all canoes. A 30 litre barrel is ideal for protecting and keeping these items dry.

Loading your canoe

Canoeists normally have one small day bag per boat to hold things like hats, gloves, lunches, drinks and an extra fleece so that they don't have to open up their barrel or large dry bag while out on the water.

Barrels and bags can be tied down to ensure they don't roll around or move about the boat – this also helps keep everything fastened to the canoe in case of capsize. A spare paddle, canoe poles and sail may also be kept out so they're handy but just make sure they don't get in the way or stop you from being able to get out. Ideally your kneeling area should be kept clear should you require a quick exit.

Remember, the more you take, the more you will have to portage around the lock gates! Don't forget to pump up your trolley wheels before you leave.

Loading your sea or touring kayak

When loading a sea or touring kayak you need to make all of your personal items, food, cooking equipment and tents fit into your kayak in the best possible way. The deck hatches on a kayak are generally watertight. However it is best to put valuable items and dry kit into dry bags just to be safe.

When packing a sea kayak, many small dry bags are more useful than a few larger bags as they allow you to fit the small bags and kit in the bow and stern of the boat. Larger items can then be fitted in the larger areas within the hull and small kit bags can fill the spaces and voids.

It's like a big jigsaw puzzle without a picture or one of those baby toys where you have to fit the right shape into the right space! Rolled up tents and tent poles fit neatly into the bow and stern sections. Sleeping bags, sleeping mats and spare clothing can all be stowed away as they only need to be taken out at camp. If any water leaks into your kayak hatches any dry kit can be sandwiched in the middle/top layer so they are not sitting in a puddle of water all day. If you want to keep things dry, put them inside dry bags to be really sure.

Remember to think about your balance and trim too. Heavy items should be placed low and central in the hatches. Too much weight in the bow or stern hatch will affect your trim and reduce your control of the boat. If you are using a deck-mounted compass for navigation, be careful where you put metallic objects!

Sea kayakers can place essentials and their lunch into their day hatch, in a small dry bag under their deck elastics or behind the seat for easy access. In windy conditions the less kit you have on your decks, the less you will be affected by the cross-winds and it will be easier for rescuers to recover your boat and empty it of water. Weight on top of your deck raises your centre of gravity making it a little more difficult to roll too.

Loading your touring paddleboard

Twelve to thirteen foot touring boards usually have two sets of deck bungees. The front deck area just forward of centre can accommodate dry bags of approximately 60–100 litres and help keep the nose down when paddling allowing the paddler to be back of centre. The rear deck area can hold a 20–40 litre bag easily. This may sound a lot but do pack as a group and try to reduce your kit baggage and weight as this will save valuable time at portage points. A small 5–10 litre dry bag is also handy for holding bits and bobs required when out on the water. This will save you having to open the larger bags and risk getting dry kit wet.

Tip: Take time to learn how to close your canoe barrels and dry bags properly – getting into a dry sleeping bag at night really does make the trail a lot more enjoyable!

Portage ▶ **verb** carry (a boat or its cargo) between navigable waters.

– ORIGIN late Middle English: from French, from *porter* 'carry'. The sense relating to carrying between navigable waters dates from the late 17th century.

(Oxford Dictionary of English)

Portage distances (travelling west to east)

WEST DISTRICT

Loch Linnhe (Corpach)	to	Corpach Upper	500m
Banavie Lower	to	Banavie Upper	650m
Gairlochy Middle	to	Gairlochy Upper	350m
Gairlochy Lower	to	Gairlochy Upper	650m

MIDDLE DISTRICT

Laggan Bay	to	Laggan Upper	250m
Cullochy Upper	to	Cullochy Lower	200m
Kytra Upper	to	Kytra Lower	200m
Ft Augustus Upper	to	Oich Pier	750m

EAST DISTRICT

Dochgarroch Upper	to	Dochgarroch Lower	200m
Torvean Upper	to	Tomnahurich Lower	400m
Muirtown	to	Caley Inn Car Park	350m
Muirtown	to	Seaport Marina	600m
Clachnaharry Works	to	Beauly Firth (Clachnaharry)	350m

Note: When passing through Gairlochy outwith lock keeper hours (0900–1700, April to September), the lower lock gates are closed overnight and a longer portage route is required from Gairlochy Lower.

Ninety-nine percent of paddlers following the Canoe Trail are content to start at Banavie Upper and finish at the Canoe Trail car park at Muirtown. During the Banavie Lower to Upper portage, a 40mph main road is crossed. At the Muirtown to Seaport Marina portage a 30mph main road is crossed and a railway line is crossed at the Clachnaharry Works to the Beauly Firth portage.

Tip: We highly recommend NOT including these sections in your paddle. However, they can be very easily walked for those who wish to have their pictures taken beside the start and finish of the Caledonian Canal to prove a coast to coast across Scotland route has been completed.

📷 *Portage team in action at Cullochy. Photo | Donald Macpherson*

Portage

Portaging is all part of the journeying skills when crossing watersheds or linking water systems to get to your destination. On the Caledonian Canal there are eleven portages on the full coast to coast route and eight on the recommended trail from Banavie Upper to Muirtown. The number of portages you will have depends on where you start and finish the trail. For those with white water experience, paddling one or more of the rivers will cut out a few portages. We only encourage this for those who are suitably skilled and experienced. Paddling a loaded craft in moving and white water can be extremely difficult as the craft has much more momentum and is harder to control.

There are many ways to portage but the technique used depends on the craft and the circumstances. How many people and craft are in the group? Are you travelling light or heavy (one small day bag or multiple large bags)? How far and over what sort of terrain? You'll have to consider all of these factors when getting ready to portage.

To assist your portages on the canal, the project has funded seventeen low-level pontoons and improved three natural landing areas near the lock gates to make it easier to get in and out of the water. The Canoe Trail portage points are clearly marked with signage on the pontoons.

The easiest method of getting out of your craft and onto one of these low-level pontoons is to first paddle alongside, then the paddler shifts over to sit on the pontoon with their feet still holding the craft against the edge. If paddling tandem, the second paddler then does the same. Emptying some of the heavier

📷 One of six stand alone low-level pontoons.
Photo | Peter Sandground Photography

📷 Sea kayak portage straps in use. Photo | Malcolm Wield

bags from a canoe or paddleboard onto the pontoon or the side of the towpath will make it light enough for you to lift it out of the water and onto the pontoon.

If travelling light, and physically able, a canoeist may opt to put their day bag on their back and carry their canoe on their shoulders using the yoke. Tandem paddlers may opt to carry the canoe together with one at the bow and the other at the stern. To prevent injury, this could also be increased in bigger groups to four paddlers positioning themselves around the boat. This makes for lighter carrying but does double the amount of walking and manual handling.

Over longer distances a canoe portage trolley is highly recommended. More accidents happen when people are tired and you may already have paddled some way before you get to the portage point.

Tip: We strongly advise all groups coming to the Great Glen Canoe Trail to bring trolleys (one per two canoes/kayaks minimum).

There is a definite skill to portaging efficiently and securing your trolley. Where bags are placed in your canoe makes a big difference to the process. The best option is to reduce the weight as much as possible by carrying a dry bag on your back. A lighter canoe requires less effort and makes portaging quicker.

When portaging with sea kayaks there are a few differences over canoe portaging. As most people use solo sea or touring kayaks you will need to pair up to lift the loaded craft off the water and onto the pontoon/portage trolley.

Not all canoe trolleys can be used to move sea kayaks due to the difference in hull shape. It is best to use a specific kayak trolley to ensure a good fit and make your portage easier. Again we advise all groups doing the Great Glen Canoe Trail to bring their own trolleys at a minimum of one trolley per two sea kayaks.

If you don't have a trolley you can always portage the sea kayak by carrying it. However, a loaded boat can be heavy and we would

📷 *Lining sea kayaks through Cullochy Locks. Photo | Donald Macpherson*

recommend the use of portage straps. Using portage straps requires two to four people, so it can lighten the load and risk. It also means that your portage will take two to four times longer than if you each had your own trolley. Portaging touring paddleboards is generally easy. Once all the bags are unloaded, the light inflatable boards can be lifted out. As touring boards are long and light, they are susceptible to the wind and could take off. Take care not to place the boards upright and then place heavy objects on the deck as this can bend the fin or even snap the fin box.

Lining through the locks

Lining is a traditional skill used for going both up and down stream. The lock keepers on the Caledonian Canal are happy to allow rafted craft to pass through the single locks at Cullochy, Kytra and Dochgarroch (if paddling west to east) and at South Laggan (if paddling east to west).

Lining will only be allowed if it doesn't affect the flow of boats moving through the waterway and is carried out safely. If the locks are busy or the weather is bad, lining through the locks might not be possible. All paddlers should be prepared to portage around all lock chambers using the low-level pontoons or natural landing points. Please remember, in all cases, it is the lock keeper's decision whether you can line through or not.

You may be allowed to line through some specified locks because the lock chamber is already flooded before you take your craft into it. Loch Oich is the highest point of the trail so when travelling away from the watershed to the coast, rafted craft can be lined into the flooded lock chamber. Once in the chamber the upper lock gates are closed over. Slowly the water is released from the chamber and when the water level equalises, the lower lock gates are opened and craft can move on through the canal. When travelling in the opposite direction the lock chamber has to be flooded. This makes the chamber turbulent with strong currents and boils and can cause issues for smaller craft.

Safety and communication

To help orientate and inform paddlers taking on the Canoe Trail, orientation panels are installed close to all access points. These

Conditions of lining through the lock chambers:

The group leader must ask the local lock keeper if it is possible to line their craft through the lock chamber and gain permission to do so (you will be required to show your canoe registration).

Rafts should then be set up in the time frame set by the lock keeper to ensure other waterway traffic is not delayed. All craft in the raft should be tied together securely using a painter at both the bow and stern of the raft. Clipping a line onto both the bow and stern on the middle craft within the raft will help move the raft into the chamber and help to control the raft as the water level drops (Two throw-bags of approx. 20m are suitable for each raft of two to four craft). Please obey any instructions given by the lock keeper to help speed up the locking process.

If a group of sea kayaks or paddleboards is given permission to line through the lock chamber, a rope should be passed under and secured on both the bow and stern to ensure a stable platform is created.

No one should be on the raft during lining through the lock chamber. All loose items should be removed from the raft and any baggage and other items left aboard should be tied down. This prevents loss of valuables and saves time if there is a capsize.

Two paddlers from the group (wearing buoyancy aids) should control the lines from the side of the lock chamber while the rest of the group keeps a safe distance from the edge of the lock chamber.

There are various reasons why lining may not be possible. Priority must always be given to those in motor craft and sailing boats who pay handsomely to navigate through the Caledonian Canal. The lock keeper may have other responsibilities to tend to in the local area and will not operate the lock unless a licensed craft needs to go through. If a paddling group is not ready in time, the lock keeper may decline permission to line through the lock chamber to keep the waterway traffic moving. For operational reasons the local District Supervisor or Canal Manager may suspend the rights to line craft through the single lock chambers.

panels highlight what's coming next on your trail, whether you are heading west or east. They also feature the facilities and services available locally including toilet facilities, camping areas, rubbish bins, shops and more. Linking in with the orientation panels, guide maps for the Canoe Trail have also been produced. These maps, which highlight features of the trail, are designed to be used alongside an Ordnance Survey Landranger map. The maps will be issued to all groups when they register with the Caledonian Canal Office and are also available as a download from www.greatglencanoetrail.info

At the time of writing (June 2020) the panels at Dochgarroch Lower, Seaport Marina and Clachnaharry works were missing.

Pre-trail practice

Taking on the Great Glen Canoe Trail is a serious challenge. Paddling a few miles is more exercise than some people normally do in a month. To best enjoy your trail adventure a little pre-trail training is highly recommended. Remember the trail is going to be a test of fitness, endurance and stamina over three to five days. Before you arrive in the Great Glen it would be advisable to get out paddling as a group to increase your paddle fitness as well as to practise some basic safety and rescue skills. Your local canoe club instructor will be able to give you advice on preparing for paddling open water.

Some things that are certainly going to make things easier:

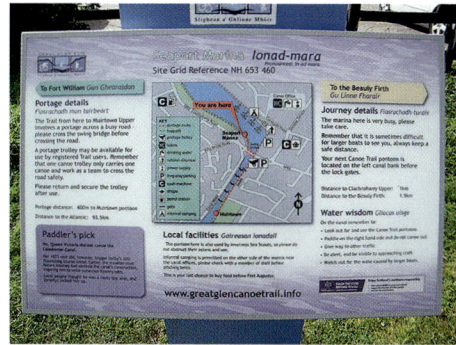

Orientation panel. Photo | Donald Macpherson

The waterproof Guide Map. Photo | Donald Macpherson

Get out and paddle a canoe, paddleboard or kayak like the one you are going to use. This will not only get you used to paddling the craft, it will help you gauge your current fitness level.

If paddling as a tandem, ensure that you get out and paddle with your partner. The last place you want to be learning to work as a team is on a busy waterway or on an open water loch.

Plan the best way to load and launch your boat at the start of each day and how to land at the end of the day.

Working out how to set up a portage trolley for your own craft is also useful.

Most importantly, practise a few emergency situations where you capsize and require assistance from your fellow paddlers and practise helping others in a rescue.

Get out and paddle with the group you intend to go with. Ensure there is a delegated leader and that the group stays together and looks after each other. Personal issues or concerns should be sorted out before taking on the trail or resolved off the water. It has been known for individual paddlers to split off on their own resulting in the group calling out emergency services as they were worried about an individual's safety.

If you are in any doubt about your skills and abilities, get some more practice or consider some personal skill development through your local club or instructors.

Groups that take on the Great Glen Canoe Trail should be aware of the likely risks and ensure they can manage these risks themselves. You can't rely on outside help in an emergency. There is only one voluntary lifeboat stationed on Loch Ness and they do need time to mobilise and to get to you. In extreme weather conditions the lifeboat crew may be unable to launch at all.

Remember you can always join in with a planned trip run by a commercial operator. Being guided through the Great Glen not only improves your local knowledge, but makes your adventure much safer.

Cold water immersion

A number of factors can greatly affect a paddler who is exposed to the elements in the great outdoors. Age, gender, fitness level, health, injury, type and colour of clothing, environment and whether they've taken any alcohol or drugs (including prescribed medication) can all greatly influence the paddler's ability to cope with situations.

Some of these factors can be taken into account when planning the trail but all group members must work well as a team and look after each other. Individuals must also take responsibility and let the group know if they need help before any situation gets out of hand. However, this isn't always possible – one side-effect of hypothermia is the inability to realise and act on what's happening, so the group must keep an eye on each other and speak out if they think someone is showing signs, such as blue-tinged fingertips and lips,

Canoeists practising rescue skills with a loaded canoe in sheltered waters before taking to the trail.
Photo | Donald Macpherson

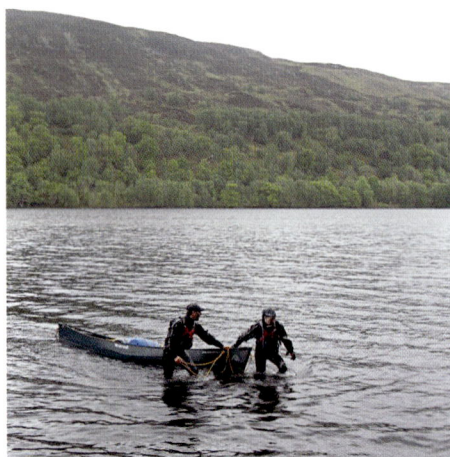

not being able to keep up, seeming unusually quiet or not contributing to the group.

One of the main risks paddlers take on is how to rescue and look after one or more casualties in an incident. Cold water is a very serious risk. Even in warm weather the water temperatures in the Great Glen can be very cold, especially in the lochs. Due to the sheer volume of water it holds, the temperature of Loch Ness stays fairly constant all year at only 6-10 degrees Celsius. In summer the top six inches occasionally warms up a little due to heat from the sun, and in winter it never freezes. Considering that body temperature is 37 degrees Celsius and the body cools 35 times more quickly in water than in air, paddlers who fall into water don't have long before the cold takes effect.

The symptoms of cold water immersion include cramp, shortness of breath, panic and fatigue. These have to be dealt with promptly and paddlers should be removed from the water as soon as possible.

The wearing of appropriate outdoors/paddling clothing will help reduce the impact of cold water immersion, gaining them valuable time to either self-rescue or get help from other group members. Just because someone is a good swimmer doesn't mean they can swim fully clothed in a cold loch.

Paddling close to the loch side can help reduce the risk of hypothermia as the capsized paddler(s) will spend less time in the water and be able to reach land quickly to find shelter, change out of wet clothing and regain vital warmth.

A good buoyancy aid and appropriate paddling clothing will save your life if you capsize. Remember, anyone can fall in at any time.

Understanding buoys

It is important to stay safe when paddling through areas used by bigger boats. Always stay clear of the deep water channels when approaching harbours and in other buoyed

Canoeists approaching the Oich Weir with caution and using the navigation markers for safety Photo | Donald Macpherson

areas. Sailors find their way into port using buoys and transits to stay in the deep water channel. In channels, most boats are restricted in their ability to manoeuvre because if they change course they may run aground. Stay outside the deep water channel to avoid being run down! The buoys on the Caledonian Canal are marking the navigation channels towards the major harbour at Inverness.

Port markers are painted RED, shaped like a tin can and are kept to port (left) as ships make their way up the channel into the harbour.

Starboard markers are GREEN, cone-shaped and are kept to starboard (right) as ships make their way into the harbour.

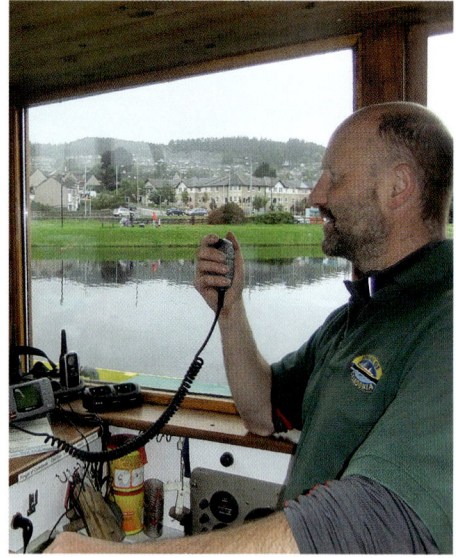

VHF radio in use on the canal. Photo | Donald Macpherson

Communication in the Great Glen

Due to the geographical nature of the Great Glen there are a few areas where there is no mobile phone or VHF coverage. Most mobile networks receive coverage at the main centres, including Fort William, Fort Augustus and Inverness. Mobile coverage can be patchy along the shoreline and bays of Loch Ness.

HM Coastguard covers the Caledonian Canal with the assistance of Scottish Canals who control the navigation from coast to coast. HM Coastguard operates both via telephone and VHF radio (see inside front cover).

When planning your Canoe Trail, you should remember to register your plan with HM Coastguard as well as obtaining a canoe registration through the Caledonian Canal office. If you'd like to access the internet from your phone, there are Wi-Fi hot spots at key locations along the route, including Corpach, Banavie, Gairlochy, South Laggan, Fort Augustus, Dochgarroch and Seaport Marina. This enables you to pay to access the internet.

What to do in an emergency

If you require rescue or emergency assistance when out on the Canoe Trail, you can summon the emergency services by dialling 999 on your phone. The police can liaise with HM coastguard and other appropriate rescue services.

Alternatively, if you have a VHF handheld radio, you can contact HM Coastguard directly on Emergency Channel 16. VHF coverage on the Caledonian Canal is good. If you can't communicate directly with the Coastguard, Caledonian Canal staff and many other commercial craft in the area also use VHF and

📷 *RNLI crew chatting to paddlers during a training exercise on Loch Ness. Photo | John Macpherson Photography*

should be able to come to assist and/or relay on your 'Mayday' as a 'Mayday Relay'.

Loch Ness is also home to Scotland's only inland Royal National Lifeboat Institution station, located just outside Drumnadrochit. Crewed and operated entirely by local volunteers, it offers a 24-hour search and rescue service carried out under the direction of the coastguard based in Aberdeen.

The water in Loch Ness is considerably colder than in UK coastal areas making it vital that you get out of the water as fast as possible after an incident.

Giving your location

When communicating with any emergency service it is extremely useful to be able to give them precise details of your group situation, numbers and exact location. Using a standard Ordnance Survey Landranger Map you should be comfortable giving a six figure grid reference.

At a scale of 1:50,000, a six-figure grid reference narrows down the emergency search to an area of 100m^2. Remember to state that you're in the Great Glen, before quoting your National Grid identification letters and your six-figure grid reference. These letters can be found on your map corners and change every 100km. This will speed up any rescue and may save lives. For example: NH 438 145 (boat house on south shore of Loch Ness).

If you're not able to make an emergency call, use your Ordnance Survey map to identify either a more suitable place to gain network coverage or locate where you may find suitable shelter off the water and access to a landline to call for assistance.

The Caledonian Canal

Welcome to the
waterway through
the Great Glen

Coast to Coast

Now you're almost ready to take to the trail ... have a look at the paddling descriptions and trip options in the following sections to help plan your adventure. It'll give you a steer on distances, environment, facilities and attractions along the way and ideas for different trips if the whole coast-to-coast route isn't for you this time.

The Great Glen Canoe Trail can be completed in various ways – specific trail routes are deliberately not given for the lochs, so that each trail will be a new experience. Most groups start the trail in the west (taking into account the prevailing wind) and plan to take between three to five days to complete. This gives plenty of time (weather dependent) to explore the Great Glen both on and off the water.

We have broken the trail into five days. As you may need a shuttle at the start and/or end, we have reduced the distance paddled on days one and five. This leaves plenty of options for groups to plan their route, where they aim to camp or book accommodation, see the local sites and ensure they are ready at appropriate times to return hired equipment and catch any flights or departing transport links from Inverness.

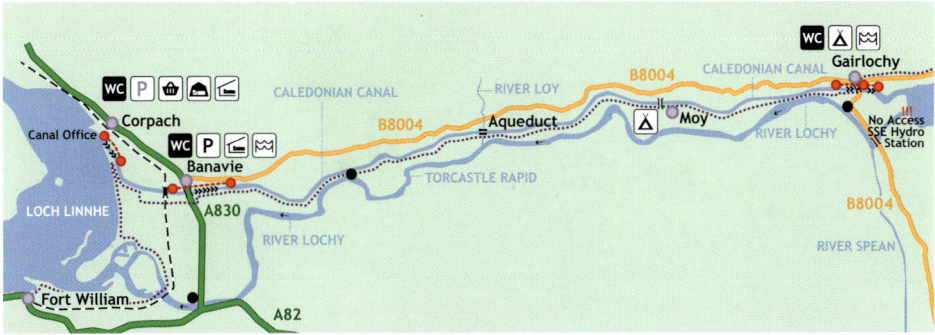

Day 1

Fort William to Gairlochy

Distance   10.5km

Grade   A – canal

OS Sheets   41 & 34

Start   NN 115 773 (Banavie Upper)

Finish   NN 179 844 (Gairlochy Upper)

Portage   NN 177 843 to 179 844 (Gairlochy Locks) 350m

Canal Office, Corpach   NN 096 767

Drop Off/Pick Up Point   NN 115 773

Long Stay Parking   NN 112 769

Welcome to the first day of your Canoe Trail adventure! The trail is yours to explore but before you take to the water please make sure you have registered for the trail online (at least 7 days in advance) at www.greatglencanoetrail. info or at the Caledonian Canal office (Corpach) or Seaport Marina (Inverness). Registering online will speed up your departure as the paperwork is already done. You'll just need to buy your facilities key and access codes at the Caledonian Canal office.

The main trail car park and pick-up point is in Banavie at the bottom of the Neptune's Staircase locks. You can leave a car here for the duration of your paddle.

Although the canal starts or ends at Corpach by Loch Linnhe, the recommended Canoe Trail begins at Banavie Upper, at the top of

39

📷 *The Jacobite steam train passing over the canal at Banavie. Photo | John Macpherson Photography*

the Neptune's Staircase flight of locks. Here you'll find an orientation panel that details the route and gives safety information about paddling on the canal. This is by the Canoe Trail Changing Area. You can access this area using the code given to you by the Canal team along with the facilities key.

Please remember to follow the paddling guidelines when using the canal – keep to the right, allow larger or faster boats to pass you and ensure that you can always be seen by other canal users.

From the vantage point at Banavie Upper there are fantastic views to the south of Loch Linnhe and to the east of Britain's highest mountain, Ben Nevis. At 1,345 metres, Britain's highest mountain is an imposing presence that towers over the town of Fort William. Every year around 110,000 people walk to the summit of 'The Ben'.

Although the canal feels peaceful and remote fairly quickly after leaving Banavie, this is still a busy stretch of water so be aware of other canal users and watch out for the wake from larger vessels.

Around 7km from Banavie, the Glen Loy Aqueduct (NN 149 818) offers the ideal opportunity for a scenic break and the chance to stretch the legs. A short walk from the canal towpath takes you to the only aqueduct on the canal. At 7.6m (25 ft) its central arch is wide enough to let the River Loy flow safely beneath the canal even when it is in spate.

Just a kilometre or so further along the canal brings the opportunity to appreciate some more fine 19th-century engineering at Moy Bridge (NN 162 826). Built in 1812, this is the only remaining original swing bridge on the canal. This elegant piece of cast-iron machinery is still hand-operated by the bridge keeper using the old winch mechanism.

There are two options as you paddle towards the picturesque crossing at Gairlochy and the finish point for day one:

1. If the lower lock chamber gates are open (during the summer season when there

is a lock keeper on duty) you can paddle through to the middle chamber and egress on the shingle beach on the north side, opposite the Thomas Telford House. The easiest way to get the canoes out of the water and up the bank to the towpath is to first take your baggage up, then work as a team (ideally in fours) to lift the canoes up to the towpath. Use the Gairlochy Middle Orientation Panel to guide your 350m portage to Gairlochy Upper.

2. If the lower lock gate is closed, paddlers can use the low-level pontoon located at Gairlochy Lower to help get out of the canal. This does add an extra 300m to the portage (including crossing the B8004 and opening two gates) but may be a more suitable option for groups that would prefer an easier egress, even when the lower lock gate is open.

Accommodation

If you're ready to set up camp for the night, there is an area for informal camping by the canal here, but space is limited. Please leave no trace of your stay and only light camp fires in the fire pit.

Visit www.greatglencanoetrail.info for the up-to-date list of B&Bs and hotels in the area. The orientation panels also give information on where to find other facilities. Don't forget word of mouth – if lock keepers are on duty, they may be able to offer valuable advice and information. Please read and follow any informal camp area guidelines set by the canal staff.

Thomas Telford

Renowned engineer Thomas Telford liked the idea of linking existing lochs and sea-lochs by canal. He saw that a canal would provide a safer east-to-west route for fishing boats than braving the open water around the coast, and create desperately needed work. This massive Highland job creation scheme lasted 19 years. The canal was finally opened in 1822 and is now a Scheduled Ancient Monument enjoyed by over half a million visitors a year.

Corpach to Banavie

If you've got your heart set on completing the whole trail from coast to coast, you'll want to start your trip at Corpach rather than Banavie. This may be a suitable option if you are in a small group and are experienced at portaging. However, the two long portages and the need to cross a very busy 40mph main road makes this section unadvisable for large or inexperienced groups.

Starting off at the canal office at Corpach this 500m portage takes you across the canal car park to Corpach Upper. Use your Scottish Canals facilities key to unlock the two gates leading to the canal (remembering to close and relock them behind you) and you'll see a Canoe Trail launching platform just past the

Crossing the main road with caution at Banavie. Photo | John Macpherson Photography

lock gate on the north side that allows easy access onto the canal.

This 1.5km section can be busy with boats heading in and out of the Caledonian Canal so be aware of larger vessels and stick to the right if busy. Paddle up and under the rail bridge to the Canoe Trail platform, located on the north side of the canal. There's some space at the far side of the towpath where you can re-group, rest and prepare for the road crossing.

If you're lucky you'll see the romantic Jacobite steam train on its way to Mallaig for one of the world's most scenic railway journeys. This train is now well known as the Hogwarts Express, as featured in the Harry Potter films. Be extremely careful crossing the road – this is a busy main road with a 40mph speed limit. Check that the towpath gate to Neptune's Staircase on the other side is open before crossing.

The best and safest way to cross is to work as a team with one person monitoring the traffic and the rest of the team lifting the craft across one at a time.

Once you're all safely across the road, the 650m portage to Banavie Upper is a bit of a trek up the side of the Neptune's Staircase locks. At the top you'll find good canal facilities that include toilets, drinking water and showers.

Portaging the double lock chamber at Corpach.
Photo | John Macpherson Photography

Day 2

Gairlochy to Loch Oich

Distance   22km

Grade   C – Loch Lochy   B – Loch Oich

OS Sheets   34

Start   NN 179 844 (Gairlochy Upper)

Finish   NN 327 013 (Leiterfearn Trailblazer Rest)

Portage   NN 285 963 to 287 966 (Laggan Locks) 250m

Day two of your adventure provides your first taste of open water paddling on the trail. Launching at Gairlochy Upper you have just under a kilometre of canal paddling before entering beautiful Loch Lochy, paddling past the second of the trail's three quaint pepper pot lighthouses on your way.

Loch Lochy is the third deepest loch in Scotland. It may be relatively narrow at just over a mile wide, but the wind can funnel down through the Great Glen from Fort William and create short dumping waves that can easily swamp a canoe or capsize a kayak. Stay close to shore to be certain you can take shelter or get out quickly if you need to.

Most paddlers follow the secluded north shore. The towering mountains and native woodland create a peaceful feel but there are other people using the loch – keep an eye out for people fishing in the Bunarkaig area. There is a fish farm located on the south west side on Loch Lochy (NN 193 854), and paddlers should where possible paddle around the outside of this area. Look out for bigger boats travelling through the same stretch. Depending on wind strength and direction, you can make up time and save energy by sailing to the Kilfinnan area.

The land between Loch Lochy and Loch Arkaig is home to the historic seat of the Clan Cameron. The Clan Cameron museum at Achnacarry is a mile or so from the shore at Bunarkaig. This area is also famous as the base for commando training during World War Two.

You may be lucky enough to see an osprey in the Great Glen, especially around Loch Lochy and Loch Ness. Be careful where you stop, and ask for local advice if you are considering wild camping in this sensitive area.

Ospreys

Seen from below ospreys are white with black patches on the wings and could be mistaken for a large gull. Ospreys were hunted to near extinction by the early 20th century but their numbers are now steadily growing in Scotland.

An osprey on the lookout from it's tree top nest.

Photo | Forestry Commission Picture Library / Neill Campbell

Road access along the north shoreline stops at the small settlement of Clunes but there are many places you can stop to stretch your legs if needed. From Clunes the land belongs to Forestry Commission Scotland and as long as paddlers follow the Scottish Outdoor Access Code (see details on page 73), camping is permitted along the shoreline.

Now is a great time to take it a bit easier on the trail. Depending on wind conditions, Loch Lochy provides an ideal environment for some sailing. Setting up your downwind sail before launching on day two will give your arms a rest and add a whole new dimension to your Canoe Trail experience (see sailing section on page 88 for guidance).

After a full morning's paddling (and perhaps sailing), Glas-dhoire Trailblazer Rest (NN 254 933) is the perfect spot to enjoy a well-deserved lunch break.

If you've been sailing, prepare to take down your sail as you arrive at the end of Loch Lochy, before Kilfinnan Point since Ceann Loch at Laggan Locks can be busy with motor boats and other canal traffic. Keep as close as possible to the green marker buoys to ensure that you follow the navigation channel guidance and can see oncoming traffic. Once around Kilfinnan Point, you can cut across the navigation channel when it is safe to do so.

Paddle round the pontoons on the north side of the canal and egress at the beach area behind Ivy Cottage (GR: NN 285 963). Do read the Canoe Trail map here as many paddlers head for the pontoon at the entrance to the canal. Getting out at the beach is a shorter and easier portage. There is a 250m portage from here around the back of Laggan Locks. You'll find an orientation panel giving information on the area. Laggan Upper marks the high point of the trail – it's all downhill paddling from here!

This could be a good time for a tea and comfort break. You may wish to visit the Eagle Barge (a converted Dutch steel barge that has been converted into a floating pub/restaurant). If you're planning on stopping for a while please ensure that your canoes and kit are moved up above the canal towpath out of the way. The road provides access to a commercial sailing company's car park – please don't block it.

Portage along the north towpath and access the water via the low-level pontoon at the far end.

The next 2.5km stretch on the canal is stunning, with trees lining and overhanging the canal and an array of colours to enjoy, especially in autumn.

Approaching Laggan Swing Bridge. Photo | Donald Macpherson

It can be busy here – remember to keep in to the right and let faster craft pass.

As the canal opens out, you will see Laggan Swing Bridge ahead. Paddlers can safely paddle under this swing bridge when it is closed over. If the bridge is open or opening, please hold back and allow motorboats to go through first, as this will reduce the amount of time cars have to wait on the busy A82 main road.

Passing under Laggan Swing Bridge takes you into the beautiful Loch Oich, the second smallest of the four lochs in the Great Glen. The Great Glen Water Park on the south shore of the loch is a popular spot for water sports. Watch out for water-skiers and give them plenty of space!

The Well of the Seven Heads is 1.5km on from here NN 305 991. The memorial on the shore marks a gruesome episode in a bloody clan feud. This place doesn't just have history – it's also a great oppor-tunity to top up your caffeine and energy levels by visiting Loch Oich Food Co. by the loch side. The café is a family run business and yes they do offer fantastic cakes and snacks. Currently they are open weekdays 6am to 2pm.

The end of day two at Leiterfearn Trailblazer Rest is approx. 2km from here.

Depending on wind strength and direction, you can make up time and save energy by sailing to Invergarry Castle.

Take care on the section between Invergarry Castle and Glengarry Castle Hotel as the loch narrows here and the waters are quite shallow, leaving very little room for larger craft to manoeuvre around smaller boats.

Once past the island you'll see the welcome site of Leiterfearn Trailblazer Rest amid beautiful native woodland on the south shore.

📷 *A scree slope on the south side of Loch Ness, an example of some of the less accessible lands in this area*
Photo | John Macpherson Photography

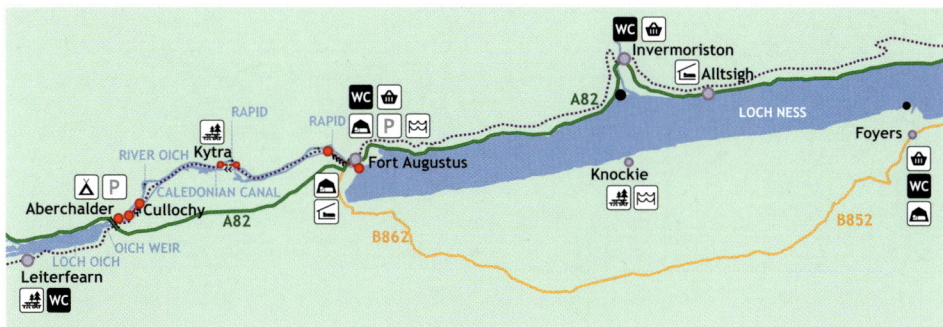

Day 3

Loch Oich to Foyers

Distance   26.5km

Grade   B – Loch Oich   C – Loch Ness

OS Sheet   34 + 26

Start   NN 327 013 (Leiterfearn Trailblazer Rest)

Finish   NH 492 211 (Loch Ness Shores Campsite, near Foyers)

Portages   NH 341 041 to 341 043 Cullochy Locks 200m

NH 352 067 to 353 068 Kytra Locks 200m

NH 376 092 to 382 093 Ft Augustus Lock Flight 750m

This is a serious day's paddling that takes you from the calm canal into the unforgiving open-water conditions of Loch Ness. Make sure you feel prepared, take rests when needed and keep your energy levels topped up.

The day starts as you launch back onto Loch Oich (the highest part of the trail) for a 2.5km paddle into Aberchalder. Be careful of the weir leading to the River Oich on your approach and keep right of the navigation marker.

At Aberchalder the A82 main road crosses the canal – paddlers can pass safely under the swing bridge when it is fully closed.

Just past the swing bridge there is a low level Canoe Trail pontoon at NH 339 037. Here you can get out, stretch your legs and read the orientation panel, visit the Old Bridge of Oich, check the River Oich level indicator and decide if you wish to paddle the river or take the much more gentle canal route.

For experienced paddlers, the River Oich is an option that avoids portages at Cullochy, Kytra and Fort Augustus, but it shouldn't be undertaken lightly. Paddling a river with a loaded canoe should only be attempted if you have white water paddling experience. Sea kayaks, paddleboards and less experienced canoeists should stick to the canal.

If you do want to run the river, it is advisable to paddle back up to the weir for a clear run down to Fort Augustus, finishing up at Loch Ness. For more details see page 68 of the river journeys section.

Most paddlers will follow the canal route and enjoy a very easy 500m paddle to Cullochy Upper – the next portage point and the first lock on the canal's descent towards the Moray Firth and the North Sea.

You'll find the low-level pontoon at the far end at the north side of the canal and the 200m portage along the towpath is fairly easy. Please remember to keep the towpath clear for canal operations and to allow Great Glen Way walkers and cyclists to pass freely.

Once you're safely back on the canal, a scenic paddle takes you to Kytra Upper. As long as it is safe to do so, please give wildlife in this area a wide berth. The swans here aren't just wild, they can be aggressive!

The portage at Kytra is again on the north towpath. If the area is busy with motorboats, paddlers can get off the water at the emergency overflow weir for the canal. There is enough space for three craft to exit here, but it does mean a slightly longer portage than from the low level pontoon. Portage 200m along the north towpath to the low-level pontoon at Kytra Lower.

The beautiful surroundings of Kytra are a lovely stopping-off point and it is a good chance to stretch your legs. If you fancy staying the night, informal camping is allowed on the other side of the canal.

The gentle paddle from Kytra Lower to Fort Augustus Upper is 3.5km.

Fort Augustus is bustling with visitors all year,

[◎] *Relaxing setting at Kytra Locks. Photo | Peter Sandground Photography*

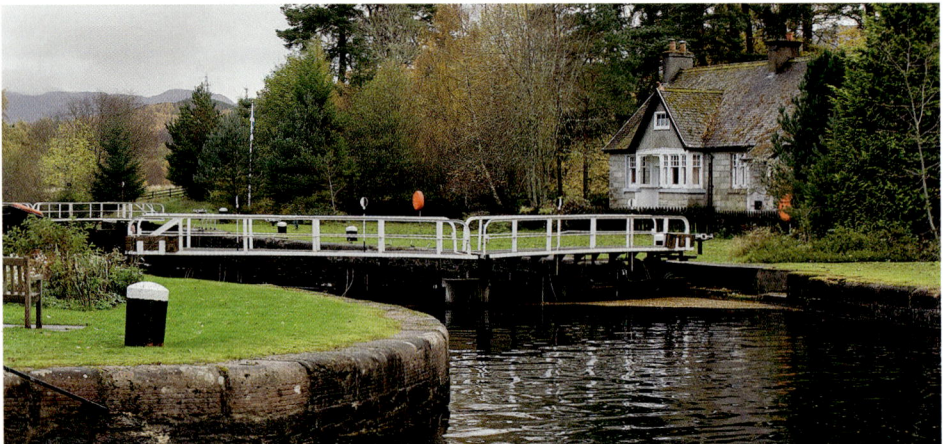

and is particularly busy in the summer season. The canal's staircase of five locks is at the heart of this picturesque village's appeal and draws many visitors to relax and watch the boats go up or down the 12 metre (40ft) change in height.

Congratulations – you've reached the halfway point of the Great Glen Canoe Trail! Give yourself a pat on the back and take time to make sure you feel properly prepared and fit before you tackle the challenge of Loch Ness.

The Canoe Trail pontoon is the last pontoon on the north side of the canal. If you are planning on portaging through Fort Augustus, this is where you should get out.

If you plan to stay in Fort Augustus overnight, a canoe rack is located on the south side beside the rubbish bin area and paddlers should get off the canal on that side to reduce the amount of lifting you have to do. There is also a small store to the left of the canoe rack where paddlers can leave paddles and some barrels, saving having to carry everything to their local accommodation. The code is the same as the Banavie Changing area given to you by the Canal team along with the facilities key. Remember your padlock to lock up your canoes and kayaks. There are Caledonian Canal toilet facilities here to the right.

When exiting at Fort Augustus Upper, please don't leave your canoes on the road as this is frequently used by cars and other vehicles. You can use the clear area near the village to rest kit and canoes while setting up your portage trolleys.

The flight of locks at Fort Augustus is the longest portage at 750m but there is good news – it's mostly downhill! When portaging down to the village please use the pavement to allow traffic to pass on the single lane road.

There is plenty to do in Fort Augustus, and lively waterside restaurants and pub. It's also a good opportunity to visit the Caledonian Canal Visitor Centre for an insight into the history and workings of the canal.

This is the main stopping point between Fort William and Inverness and a good chance to

📷 *Wee Nessie. Photo | Scott Rawstorne*

The Loch Ness Monster

The elusive Nessie has been making waves since photos taken in the 1930s made her a worldwide celebrity. The famous monster continues to attract visitors to the shores and waters of the loch in the hope of a glimpse. Keep your eyes peeled.

📷 *Limited landing spots for resting or taking shelter should conditions deteriorate. Photo | Donald Macpherson*

stock up on fresh food for the rest of the trip. From the village you need to cross the road carefully and follow the towpath down to Oich Pier. On your way down you will find rubbish bins and toilet facilities. These are your last toilets until Loch Ness Shores commercial campsite, if you are planning to stay there.

Loch Ness

At 37km long, 1.6km wide and up to 230 metres deep, Loch Ness is a serious stretch of water. Conditions on Loch Ness can be more like the open sea than inland water, with waves of over 3 metres possible in bad weather. This is why the loch is home to the only RNLI station on inland water.

Always make sure you get an up-to-date weather forecast before you set off. If in doubt – don't! Depending on the weather conditions you need to carefully plan which side of the loch to follow. The water temperature here stays between 6–10°C all year so you need to be able to get out of the water quickly if you fall in. Cold-water immersion is a serious consideration (see safety information on page 32). To help speed your progress down the loch, it is a good idea to have your sail at hand.

Loch Ness can be busy with larger boats. Cruise Loch Ness operates a number of cruise boats and fast rib-boats from Fort Augustus up to Urquhart Castle. Stay together as a group, look out for each other and make sure you're visible to fast-moving craft.

Following the south shore

The south shore is exposed and offers very few places to land or shelter. You can get out at Knockie (NH 438 145) but this is 7.5km along the loch. There are limited facilities but there is a cleared area approximately 50m up the track where you can pitch tents if you need to take shelter. If planning to stay here overnight, please use the canoe racks to stow away your canoes – this keeps the area around the private boathouse clear for access.

From Knockie, Loch Ness Shores commercial campsite NH 492 211 is a further 9km along the exposed shoreline, with only a few locations along the way that offer shelter.

At Loch Ness Shores commercial campsite, there are set areas for tent camping, toilets and shower facilities, a small shop and café. If you would like to explore the area a little more, visit the Falls of Foyers, or pop to the local village store.

The Falls of Foyers

This short but spectacular walk takes you to one of the hidden gems of Loch Ness. Follow the way-marked paths to see the spectacular waterfall cascading down a gorge into the loch.

Among the heathy hills and
ragged woods
The roaring Foyers pours
his mossy floods;
Till full he dashes on the
rocky mounds,
Where, thro' a shapeless breach,
his stream rebounds.
Robert Burns, 1787

Following the north shore

The north shore route past Cherry Island crannog offers a number of egress points between Fort Augustus and Invermoriston, 8km away. Just before you reach Invermoriston Old Pier (NH 426 157), you can take a 1km walk into the village for supplies at the village shop or to use local accommodation. The river mouth at Invermoriston is a prime spot for fishermen – please show them respect and give them plenty of space.

From Invermoriston you have a 4.5km paddle to Alltsigh, where there is the Lochside Hostel that you can walk to from the shoreline.

After Alltsigh there is little chance to land or exit the loch due to the steep sides. Your next exit is Loch Ness Shores (near Foyers) or if the weather conditions were unsuitable for crossing the loch, you could go on to Loch Ness Bay campsite just past Urquhart Castle in Borlum Bay.

Foyers Falls. Photo | Donald Macpherson

Looking back up Loch Ness from Lochend Beach.
Photo | Donald Macpherson

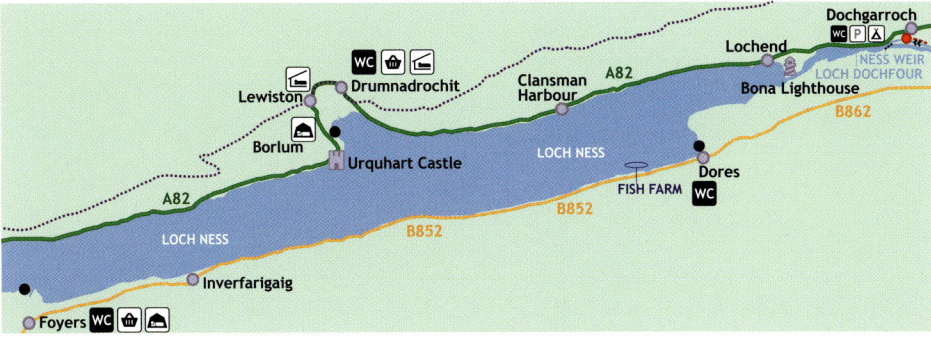

Foyers to Dochgarroch

Distance   23.5km

Grade   C – Loch Ness   B – Loch Dochfour

OS Sheets   34 & 26

Start   NH 492 211 (Loch Ness Shores Campsite)

Finish   NH 619 405 (Dochgarroch Lower)

Portage   NH 618 404 to 619 405 Dochgarroch Locks 200m

This is another big day of paddling on Loch Ness – choose either the north or south shore option until Lochend, where the trail enters Loch Dochfour. Check the weather conditions before you set off and stick to a shore once you've chosen your route.

South shore

Launching from Foyers shoreline, you have a 3.5km paddle following the south shore to Inverfarigaig pier – just the thing to get you warmed up. As you leave Foyers you'll notice

the hydro power station. Please keep a safe distance from this to avoid being caught in its outflow. It was originally built by the British Aluminium Company in 1896 and was the first large-scale commercial hydro-electric power scheme in the UK. Today it is part of a pumped-storage hydro-electricity scheme.

The disued old pier at Inverfarigaig NH 517 237 offers a sheltered bay for paddlers looking for a place to sit out bad weather or stretch their legs and explore the area.

It's a 13.5km paddle from Inverfarigaig to the

📷 *Landing well away from the jetty when visiting Urquhart Castle. Photo | John Macpherson Photography*

next stopping point at Dores beach NH 598 348. You may wish to have your sails ready to make this leg of the journey a bit easier. In windy conditions it may be safer to avoid landing at Dores beach and instead head diagonally downwind to Tor Point and make directly for Lochend/Bona lighthouse as launching back into a head wind and breaking waves from Dores beach and ferry gliding may be tricky.

Ensure that you give the fish farm just before Dores beach a wide berth and pass on the outside of the farm to avoid the ropes and cables running from the shoreline to the cages.

North shore

Following the north shore from Alltsigh, there are very few places to exit and you are really committed to paddling the full 12.5km to Urquhart Castle NH 531 286

Once one of Scotland's largest castles, the ruin of Urquhart Castle includes a tower house that gives commanding views of the famous loch and Great Glen. Its romantic appeal and fabulous setting make it an extremely popular visitor attraction. As you paddle round this stunning medieval castle, you will see a pier. This is regularly used by the large sightseeing cruise boats. Please make sure you can be seen and keep a clear distance. Craft can be landed on the shore well past the pier. Remember to pull your canoes away from the shoreline and tie the painter to a tree in case a ship's wash pulls them back into the loch.

If conditions on the loch make it unsuitable for paddling and you need to rest or stretch your legs, a trip to the castle is a worthwhile option. Historic Scotland, managers of the castle, are happy for paddlers to visit the ruin. If you wish to visit the site, and not just stay on the beach area, you should as a group report directly to the main reception where you can purchase a visitor pass ticket to explore the site.

There are toilets, a café and regular presentations on the history of the castle and area, as well as the fascinating ruins and setting to enjoy. Temple Pier at Urquhart Bay NH 530 300 is where the RNLI lifeboat is stationed.

Leaving Urquhart Bay the final leg of your journey on Loch Ness is 11.5km to Lochend/Bona lighthouse. Halfway along the trail is the Clansman Hotel where a number of the Jacobite ships operate regularly. Please give the Clansman harbour a wide berth, and if you want to use the hotel facilities you can take your canoes out of the water at the slipway just past the harbour entrance.

As you get closer to Lochend, you will see Aldourie Castle nestled in the woods. This stunning baronial style castle was first built in 1626 and is now a beautifully refurbished retreat for the well-heeled.

The 19th-century landmark, Bona lighthouse NH 602 377, was built by Thomas Telford to guide ships travelling the Caledonian Canal safely into Loch Dochfour. Famous as the UK's only inland lighthouse, it has now been given a new lease of life as it has been converted into unique holiday accommodation.

From Bona lighthouse the loch narrows and is clearly marked with red and green navigational buoys for larger boats. Port buoys are red and starboard buoys are green. The boats will pass between them, with the red

to their left and the green to their right, in the deep water channel as they head towards Inverness. Please ensure you either follow the navigation channel guidance or keep out of the marked channel when other boats are around in this busy area.

As Loch Dochfour starts to open out you'll find a sheltered bay on the south shore. A closer inspection will reveal the wrecked remains of a pair of old coal barges (NH 608 388).

Avoid the weir that forms the start of the River Ness and paddle by the green navigation buoy located just before the weir and head for the left/North side of the canal. By moving over to the left, paddlers will be away from the weir. When the loch is high and in windy conditions the weir continues to flow along the full length causing a current towards the weir drawing craft in.

You then have less than a kilometre to paddle along the canal to Dochgarroch Upper. There are many boats berthed in this area so follow the canal navigation code and paddle on the right side of the canal down to the low-level pontoon.

After using the low-level pontoon to help you get off the canal, you then have a 200m portage to Dochgarroch Lower where there is an area suitable for informal camping. This marks the end of day four and a welcome rest for weary paddlers.

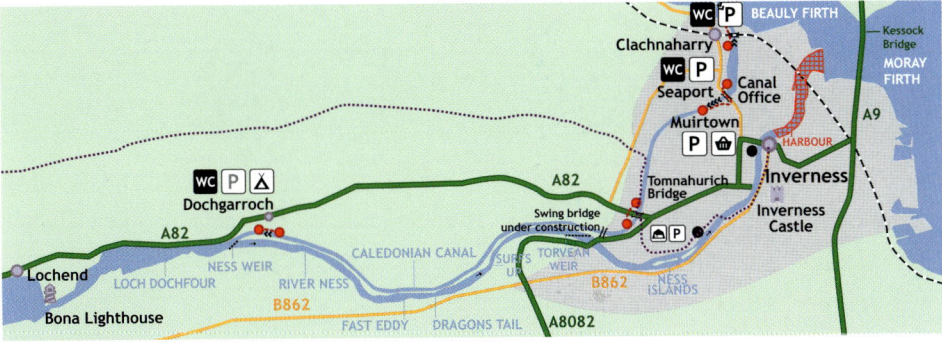

Dochgarroch to Inverness

Distance   8km

Grade   A – canal

OS Sheets   26

Start   NH 619 405 (Dochgarroch Lower)

Finish   NH 654 457 (Muirtown Car Park Pick Up Point)

Portage   NH 655 437 Torvean to 654 439 Tomnahurich 400m

NH 652 454 to 654 457 Muirtown 350m

Canal Office, Seaport   NH 654 460

Pick Up/Drop Off Point   NH 654 457

Long Stay Parking   NH 654 457

The final day of your Great Glen Canoe Trail brings you into the city of Inverness, the Capital of the Highlands. At Dochgarroch you can choose to follow the Caledonian Canal route to the finish point at Muirtown or if you have white water experience, you can paddle the River Ness right into the heart of the city (see River Ness guide on page 68). It is recommended that all sea kayakers, paddle boarders and canoeists who aren't experienced on white water follow the canal route.

If you are taking the canal route, launch back onto the water using the low-level pontoon at Dochgarroch Lower. This 5.5km stretch of water to the first portage at Torvean Upper can be very busy. Take care – you may be sharing the canal with hired motor cruisers, the Jacobite Queen sightseeing boat on her way down to and from Loch Ness and members of the Inverness Rowing Club out training. Rowers face backwards and can't see you so stay alert and keep to the right.

At Torvean and Tomnahurich Swing Bridges canoeists, paddleboarders and kayakers can paddle underneath with care when either of the bridges are fully shut. If in any doubt have a word with the Bridge Keeper first to check that they aren't about to open before attempting it. These bridges have the lowest clearance of all the swing bridges on the Calendonian Canal and you will need to tuck down to pass comfortably underneath. If you're at all unsure about your limbo abilities, you can avoid the bridges by getting out between the rowing club pontoon and the new transit boat wharf just before Torvean Swing Bridge. You can then portage the 400m from here to just past Tomnahurich Swing Bridge, where there is a low-level pontoon.

Please be careful when crossing the busy A82 main road.

The portage here involves crossing the A82, one of the Highlands' busiest roads. Take care and work as a team to get yourselves and canoes over safely.

If you fancy a break here, a short walk across to the other side of the canal takes you to the Floral Hall tearoom – a perfect spot for a refreshing cuppa in pretty surroundings. There's also a swimming pool, showers and toilets in the nearby leisure centre and a commercial campsite beside Bught Park if you decide you'd like to stop overnight.

From Tomnahurich Lower it's just 2km on to Muirtown. Keep a look out about halfway along, the Caley Marina and Caley Cruisers base to the left-hand side can be busy with boats (many helmed by first-time skippers). As there is a lot of boat activity in the area please ensure you keep to the right-hand side of the canal so other canal users can spot you easily. The end is in sight now! From Caley Marina

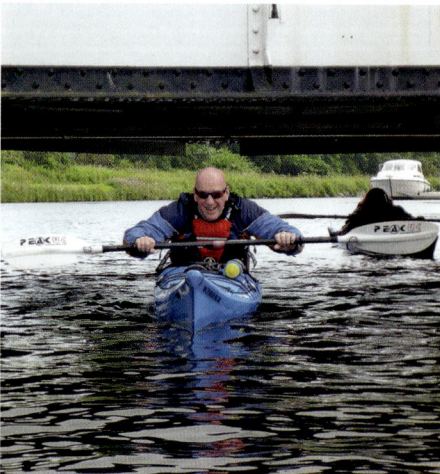

Passing safely under one of the two swing bridges at Tomnahurich, Inverness. Photo | Donald Macpherson

Inverness

Although there has been a settlement in this area since the 6th century, Inverness has really come into its own in the 21st century, becoming the UK's most northerly city in 2000. This vibrant place is growing fast – the Inverness area is home to around a quarter of the population of the Highlands.

you will get your first sight of Muirtown Lock Flight and the low-level pontoon on the right-hand side that marks the recommended end of the Canoe Trail.

It's best to finish the Trail at Muirtown because the route from here to the sea involves several difficult and dangerous portages, first across a road and then a railway line.

The Canoe Trail pick up/drop off point is an easy 350m downhill portage following the side of the lock flight. Please remember to close the towpath gates after use.

Across the road at the Caledonian Canal office at Seaport Marina you can return your facilities key. There are washing, toilet and shower facilities you can use here if required. Be sure to let staff know about your trail experience – your feedback is crucial in maintaining and improving paddler facilities.

Informal camping is permitted beside the Caledonian Canal building but please check with a member of staff before pitching tents.

Muirtown – Clachnaharry

If you have set out to do the complete Great Glen Canoe Trail from west to east coast, there is still a further 250m portage to negotiate. It's essential that you work as a team to cross the main road. The easiest place to cross with boats is at the car park exit. Once across the road you can portage your canoe along the far pavement and through the black gate onto the towpath.

The large pontoon is also used by other groups and may have motor crafts moored. As before, this area can be busy with boat traffic so take care and make sure you're visible.

Following the left-hand canal bank you have a 1 kilometre paddle to the low-level pontoon at Clachnaharry Upper.

As the last portage crosses the railway line; it's better to take your canoes out of the water here, leave them neatly at Clachnaharry Upper and walk the last 350m to the Beauly Firth. Not only will it save you an extremely difficult portage; it is also an easier location for loading up your vehicle or canoe trailer. When driving in to collect your craft and equipment, please do not block the towpath for local dog walkers, cyclists and the local business hubs. If you do want to take your canoe all the way to the sea, speak to the Network Rail Bridge Keeper first in his bothy on the left as you go through the white picket fence for train timings, and be extremely careful when crossing the railway line. You can access the Beauly Firth from the area to the left of the canal, by the final orientation panel.

For most the final portage down Muirtown Flight to the Canoe Trail car park. Photo | John Macpherson Photography

📷 *Magical Loch Ness. Photo | Donald Macpherson*

Other Options

For those of you who are relatively new to taking to the great outdoors, a single or multi-day option might be more appealing, especially for introducing young children to outdoor life.

Multi-day paddles

Neptune's Staircase to South Laggan

Distance 26.5km **Grade** C

Starting off at Banavie Upper NN 115 773 follow Day 1 & 2 route to Laggan Lower NN 285 963. Paddlers can leave a vehicle at the Highland Council car park NN 287 962.

South Laggan to Fort Augustus

Distance 15.5km **Grade** B

Starting off at Laggan Upper NN 287 966 follow Day 2 & 3 route to Fort Augustus Upper NH 376 092.

Fort Augustus to Inverness

Distance 40–48km **Grade** C

Starting off at Oich Pier NH 382 093 follow Day 3–5 route to either Dochgarroch Upper NH 618 404 or to Muirtown Upper NH 652 454. Paddlers can request permission from the canal office to leave a vehicle at the canal car park at Dochgarroch or at Muirtown Basin.

Single-day paddles

Some paddlers may not have the time or experience to take on the full Canoe Trail. Here are some other suggested routes if a day paddle is the right option for you.

Neptune's Staircase to Gairlochy

Distance   10km   Grade   A

Launching at Banavie Upper NN 115 773, you have a clear paddle along the Caledonian Canal to Gairlochy Lower NN 175 841. Stop and stretch your legs and see the engineering feat of the Loy Aquaduct or at Moy Swing Bridge, the only original swing bridge on the canal.

South Laggan to Loch Oich

Distance   4–8.5km   Grade   B

This is probably one of the most scenic canal sections of the Great Glen Way Canoe Trail. Launching at Laggan Upper NN 287 966 you paddle along the tree-lined route of Laggan Avenue. Pass under Laggan Swing Bridge and enter Loch Oich. The options are to paddle to the Well of the Seven Heads and get off the loch at the slipway this side of the pontoon NN 305 990, or paddle across Loch Oich to the low-level pontoon at Aberchalder NH 339 037.

Aberchalder to Fort Augustus

Distance   7km   Grade   A

Launching at Aberchalder NH 339 037 you have a short paddle before portaging at Cullochy Locks. Back on the canal there's a lovely 3km stretch of canal to take you to Kytra Locks. Finishing your last portage at Kytra, you can then paddle into Fort Augustus NH 376 092.

Paddle Loch Ness

Distance   33.5–40km   Grade   C

This is a long one-day paddle so take extra food, water and shelter in case you need to camp out overnight due to the weather conditions. This day paddle is more suited to experienced sea kayakers, paddleboarders and canoeists. We would strongly recommend you tandem canoe this distance. Launching from Oich Pier in Fort Augustus, you can follow Day 3 & 4 route to either Dores beach and celebrate your achievement with refreshment at Dores Inn NH 598 348, or continue on to Dochgarroch Upper NH 618 404.

OTHER OPTIONS

Surfing on the Oich Weir by Aberchalder.   Photo | John Macpherson Photography

River Journeys

This section details the three rivers that can be paddled as part of the Great Glen Canoe Trail. When paddling the trail west to east, you may choose to paddle Rivers Oich and Ness. Those who take on the trail east to west may choose to paddle the River Lochy. Please don't take these river routes unless you are experienced white water paddlers. Remember that loaded craft are harder to control on moving water as they gain momentum very easily, making them harder to run tricky rapids, slow down, and change direction.

For those who do take to the rivers with a loaded craft it makes sense to take safe routes or dry lines down stronger rapids and wave trains. This will reduce the chance of swamping your vessel and the possibility of capsizing with all your kit.

If you fancy running the rivers in a lighter craft, you can always contact a local taxi company in Fort William, Fort Augustus or Inverness to collect your baggage before starting your river trip and then collect it at your destination. Beginners and those using sea kayaks or paddleboards are advised to follow the canal.

Tip: Stay safe on the river:
- Wear your helmet and carry a throw bag.
- Ensure your kit is securely attached to your craft.
- Inspect all rapids that you are unfamiliar with before paddling them.

It is common courtesy to respect local fishermen by asking them which side of the river they would prefer you to pass by.

Contact the local river adviser for further information on the rivers. Visit the SCA website – www.canoescotland.org for a list of the current River Advisers and contact details.

📷 *Loch Oich Weir leading onto the River Oich. Photo | Donald Macpherson*

River Oich

Distance 9km
OS Sheet 34
Grade 1(2)

This river flows north-east out of Loch Oich into the south-western end of Loch Ness at Fort Augustus. The Oich flows parallel to the Caledonian Canal for much of its length and offers a more exciting alternative route into Loch Ness for experienced white water paddlers. It also avoids portages at Cullochy, Kytra and Fort Augustus. The river is fairly flat with only a handful of rapids that may require inspection by those unfamiliar with the river. The first of these is at the start of the river, which is marked by a weir where it flows out of Loch Oich. The second is just under the road bridge as the river flows to the right. Close to Kytra and just over 1km further downstream there are two more significant rapids.

Water level

The river is fairly shallow in places and needs a reasonable flow of water to avoid too much of a scrape in some sections. Water levels will vary depending on releases from the River Garry hydro-electric scheme and local rainfall.

Gauge

Look out over the A82 bridge at Bridge of Oich to check the amount of water spilling over the weir out of Loch Oich. If the whole length of the weir is covered with a stopper/wave formed along it the river will be at a good level and most of the rocks in the rapids will be covered. If only a small section, or none, of the weir is covered the rapids will be bumpy – something to be wary of if you are paddling a boat fully loaded with equipment and supplies.

Route description

This is a pleasant and straightforward paddle that allows you to take in the beauty of

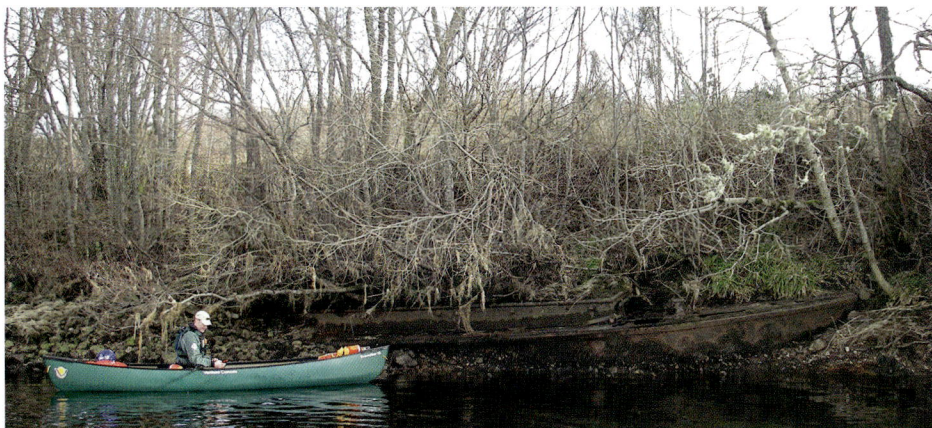

Evidence of canal repairs back in 1947 when river erosion breached the canal. Photo | Donald Macpherson

the Great Glen as you make your way down towards Loch Ness.

The banks of this river are heavily wooded in places so keep a look out ahead for trees both over-hanging the river banks and for any that might have been washed downstream.

As you are nearing Fort Augustus, be cautious of the three bridges that cross the river. Care should be taken to avoid being pushed up against any bridge stanchions/legs. The first bridge is the remains of the old railway bridge, the second is where you pass under the main A82 road bridge. The third and final bridge before entering into Loch Ness is the old disused wooden bridge. Paddlers, especially when the river is high, should plan to paddle between the middle of the stanchions to prevent broaching.

As you head towards the open waters of Loch Ness, keep close to the right-hand bank as Oich Pier is just around the corner. Here you can land your canoes, use the facilities and take a walk around the village.

Navigating the last river obstacle, Old Fort Augustus bridge, before arriving at Loch Ness. Photo | Donald Macpherson

River Ness

Distance   9km
OS Sheet   26
Grade   1/2

All the rapids can be portaged; however, there are generally dry lines on most sections of rapids that can be paddled with a loaded canoe after a quick inspection. Small surf waves and good eddy lines can be found at different locations depending on river levels and movement of rocks, but there is always something to provide some fun for the enthusiastic white water paddler.

Important info

Although the Ness weirs are regularly run, weirs are dangerous – rocks, spikes and debris are common – have a good look before you choose your route and if in doubt, line your craft down the side or portage around. Over the last year metal pilings have been put in above and below the main paddling line to reinforce the weir. In low water conditions, the Dochfour Weir is now NOT recommended with loaded craft.

Water level: This river runs all year round as it is fed from Loch Ness, but it can get a bit low in places during dry spells.

Route description

From Dochgarroch paddle up the canal to where the river starts – carry your canoe over the edge of the grassy weir where you will find a few wee streams you can safely line or float your craft down

Keep a lookout for wildlife as you paddle – kingfishers, otters and herons are among some of the species that live along the river. This is also a popular fishing river, with estate fishing as far as Torvean / Holm Mills Weir and then local angling association fishermen using the river down to the sea. Please be considerate of anglers' needs.

Also watch out for the rapids with strong eddy lines. These include Fast Eddy (river right of the first mid-river wall) and Dragons

Tail (next rapid down, river left just after the big lodge). After these entertaining rapids you'll come across a dilapidated weir that gives nice surf waves. You can paddle either side of this feature to keep your boat as dry as possible.

At Torvean / Holm Mills Weir be sure to avoid the six visible sluice gates protruding from the bank on river right. Either choose the chicken chute line (if river level permits) just a few metres left of the sluice gates, or stop a safe distance upstream from the sluice gates and portage to below them on the right-hand bank. There are other options including a trickier rapid approximately 2/3rds of the way down the weir; however, this is not recommended for inexperienced paddlers or those with loaded boats. There may be large rocks in the main chute, making it unwise to run if there is a risk of capsize. These rocks do move in flood conditions so it's always best to inspect the section before running it. This line is quite difficult to inspect if the river level is high and water flowing over the full weir. There are (at the time of writing, June 2020) plans to install an Archimedes Screw at the end of this weir to produce hydro power for the local leisure centre. Therefore building works and restrictions are likely in this area soon.

Downstream from the weir, the new bridge over the River Ness has been installed allowing the Inverness bypass route to be created. One of the new bridge stanchions is in the main river flow, but paddlers do have time to paddle around the base of the stanchion.

There are some more gentle rapids as the river runs down through the Ness Islands and into the heart of Inverness.

Once in Inverness, you can get off the river at either Fishermans car park NH 664 441 on river left just after the Ness Islands or approximately 1km further down on the left bank by The Waterfront bar NH 662 455. From here it's just a 15 minute walk to collect your car from Seaport Marina.

If you'd like to paddle the river right out into the Beauly Firth, you must get permission at least 24 hours beforehand from the Inverness Harbour Master. Call 01463 715715 for permission and important safety information before you paddle through this busy commercial port area. As the river meets the port area, just between the Black Bridge and the rail bridge, there is a more natural rocky weir. This is no issue during medium or high tide, but it is obvious and boney around low water.

Inverness Harbour is located just inside the mouth of the River Ness and when large cargo boats have to turn there is little room for them to manoeuvre in the narrow river. Once committed to turning they cannot stop due to the river flow.

Please investigate local weather conditions, river flow and tide times as these three factors are extremely important when paddling out of the river mouth and into the Beauly Firth. Be careful or your trail may end up longer than expected when you start drifting out into the inner Moray Firth or beyond!

River Lochy

Distance   10km
OS Sheet   41
Grade   1 (2/3)

The River Spean becomes the River Lochy at Mucomir Hydro-electric Power Station and offers a pleasant paddle running west towards to Fort William. This river could be used as part of the Canoe Trail for those paddling east to west or as part of a loop route. With one grade 2/3 rapid at Torcastle that must be watched out for. You can avoid this by portaging on the right-hand side over the rocks.

This run provides a gentle introduction to moving water and is suitable for open canoes and shorter touring kayaks whether loaded or not.

Water level: The river always holds water but can become fast in spate conditions.

Gauge: You can check the flow at the put-in. The first shingle rapids give a good indication of the trip.

Route description

The run consists of mainly grade 1 shingle rapids apart from one grade 2/3 on a left-hand bend at Eas nan Long (The Waterfall of the Ship), more commonly known as Torcastle.

At low water this rapid is a straightforward shoot into a pool. With more water it becomes a powerful rapid with several alternative shoots, surging boils and powerful eddy lines. The take-out is marked by the river from the outflow from the aluminium smelter. Depending on the river level, and the state of the tide, this tailrace can provide a fine play spot but is more normally a boily mess! This river has a tendency to collect tree debris which may become a hazard, particularly at high flow.

Loop routes

For more experienced paddlers looking for a one-day journey, there are a number of fantastic loops that include canal, loch and river.

Banavie to Gairlochy (returning to Fort William by river)

Distance 10km canal / 10km river

OS Sheet 41

Grade A canal & 1 (2/3)

From the top of Neptune's Staircase NN 115 773, you can follow the day one route along to Gairlochy. Taking out at either Gairlochy Lower or Middle you can portage 400m along the B8004 towards Spean Bridge (Portage trolleys recommended). There are various spots on the right side of the road where you can launch onto the River Lochy. The river will then carry you back towards Fort William. The only rapid that will definitely require inspection (and likely portage) is at the Torcastle Rapid (2/3). The river then continues past Inverlochy where you can get out on river right just after you pass under the A830 road bridge. For a slightly longer more challenging route, you could keep paddling out into Loch Linnhe and along the shore line to Corpach. The Canal Office at Corpach can advise you of local tide times for Loch Linnhe. For a shorter loop route and portage, paddle 2km along the canal from Neptune's Staircase then exit the canal and portage roughly 40m onto the River Lochy. Joining the river just below Torcastle rapid leaves a gentle 3.5km river paddle to egress river right just past the A830 road bridge.

Fort Augustus to Aberchalder (returning to Fort Augustus by river)

Distance 8km canal / 9km river

OS Sheet 34

Grade A canal & 1 (2)

From the top of Fort Augustus Locks NH 376 092, you can paddle back along the canal portaging at Kytra, Cullochy to Aberchalder NH 339 037. At Aberchalder you can assess the river level indicator and decide whether to paddle into Loch Oich and return the same way, or paddle the River Oich back down to Fort Augustus to Oich Pier NH 382 093. (See River Oich on Page 66 for more details.)

Muirtown to Loch Dochfour (returning to Muirtown by river)

Distance 9km canal / 9km river

OS Sheet 26

Grade A canal & 1/2

Launching from the top of Muirtown Locks NH 652 454 you can paddle along the canal paddling under both swing bridges to Dochgarroch Lower NH 619 405. At Dochgarroch portage around the lock gates and paddle along to the end of the canal. You can portage onto the River Ness where the canal bank stops and the River Ness weir starts.

Follow the river back down through the Ness Islands – you can get off the water here, or carry on down 1.5km through the town centre and exit on river left by The Waterfront bar NH 662 455. From here it's a 15 minute walk back up to Muirtown to collect your vehicle. (See River Ness on Page 68.)

Feral goat on the south shore of Lock Ness. Photo \ Donald Macpherson

Scottish Outdoor Access Code

Scotland is renowned for its beautiful landscapes and its diverse wildlife that attracts visitors from afar. To ensure that this fantastic asset is maintained for the future we ask all who take to the trail to treat it with respect.

Wild camping

The Land Reform (Scotland) Act 2003 gives everyone statutory access rights to most land and inland water. People only have these rights if they exercise them responsibly by respecting people's privacy, safety and livelihoods, and Scotland's environment.

Under the Scottish Outdoor Access Code (SOAC), wild camping is allowed in Scotland but you must keep to the guidelines.

Wild camping should be done in small numbers and only for a short time in any one place. If you are close to a house or building, ask the owner's permission. Take care not to disturb any wildlife especially during the breeding seasons and most importantly leave no trace. Remember, the canal is a Scheduled Ancient Monument and wild camping is not permitted on its banks.

Leave no trace

One of the key requirements of the Scottish Outdoor Access Code is that you should leave areas as you find them:

- Take all your litter away with you (including used toilet paper and any women's sanitary items).
- Remove all traces of your tent pitch and of any open fire.
- Do not cause any pollution.

Visit www.outdooraccess-scotland.com for more information on wild camping.

Human waste

Respecting the countryside also means taking care when you have to do the toilet. Each group should ensure that there are a couple of toilet bags available for use when stopping for a break/rest or setting up camp.

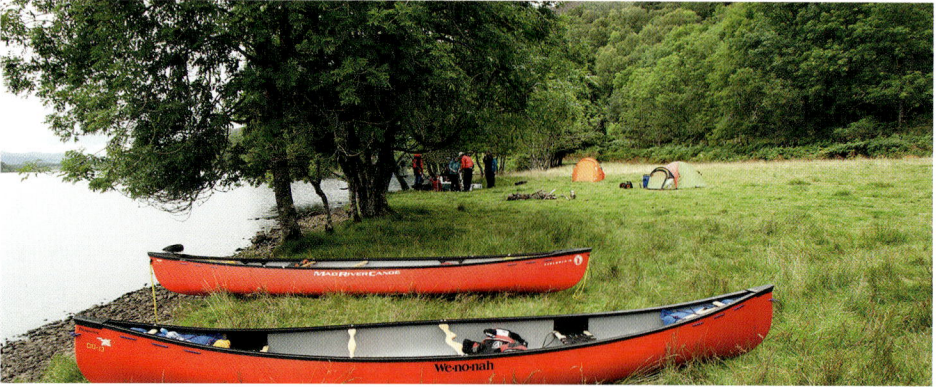

Setting up camp a Leiterfearn Trailblazer Rest, Loch Oich. Photo | Donald Macpherson

Within each toilet bag:

- A small hand trowel
- Toilet paper
- Hand wash

When you need to go in the great outdoors, follow these simple guidelines:

- Where possible use local toilet facilities throughout the Great Glen to help reduce human pollution.
- If you need to urinate, do so at least 30m away from any water sources including lochs, streams and rivers.
- If you need to defecate, do so as far away as possible from any buildings, water sources and away from any farm animals. Ensure you bury faeces in a shallow hole and replace the turf (don't bury toilet paper or tampons/towels – take these with you in a sealed bag to be disposed of in the next rubbish bin).
- Please do not go to the toilet along the canal banks.

Over 4,000 paddlers pass through each year and everyone needs to do their bit to ensure the Great Glen maintains its natural beauty.

Lighting fires

Wherever possible use a stove rather than light any campfires. At some areas like the Informal Camp Areas and Trailblazer Rests, the lighting of fires is either prohibited or controlled by designated fire pits.

All campfires should be kept small so they are easier to control, require less fuel (wood), and are easier to remove all trace of before moving on. Never light open fires during pro-longed dry periods, or in areas such as forests, woodland, farmland, or near buildings.

Much of the ground around the Great Glen is very peaty and fire can easily take hold. Use a fire pit provided, take along a fire pan if you intend to have a camp fire or locate your small fire on the stony shoreline. Unmanaged camp fires can cause major damage.

By taking a few simple precautions you can enjoy a cheerful camp fire without damaging the environment.

Campfires

The smaller the fire the lower the risk of it getting out of control. It also requires less wood and sufficient to cook off or keep a group warm on colder evenings.

Use only drift wood or what you find on the forest floor. DO NOT break or cut down branches. You may be camping in an area classified as Site of Special Scientific Interest (SSSI). Please remove all traces of your fire before you move on.

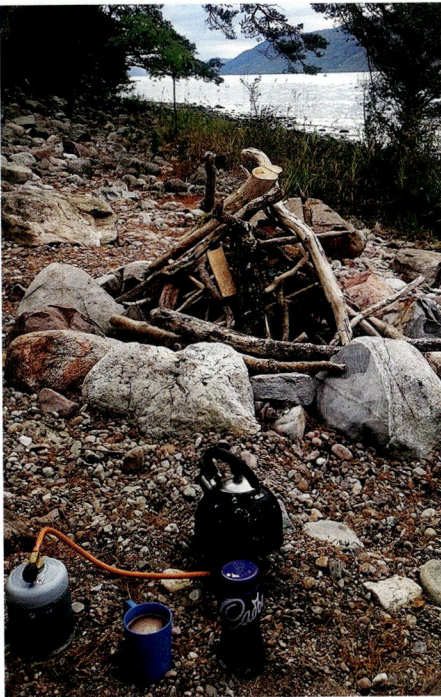

Invasive species and biosecurity

All paddlers should be aware that they may inadvertently contribute to the spreading of alien species, parasites and disease by transporting them through waterways in their boat or on their equipment. The consequences of such actions could cause significant economic problems not just for the local area, but for the nation and paddling access in general.

By taking some simple precautions this can be easily avoided. See the CHECK, CLEAN, DRY poster on page 95. Further information is also available online at www.canoescotland.org

Paddlers' Access Code

The Scottish Canoe Association have created an excellent leaflet specifically aimed to advise paddlers of their rights and responsibilities within the Land Reform (Scotland) Act. This leaflet is available at www.canoescotland.org

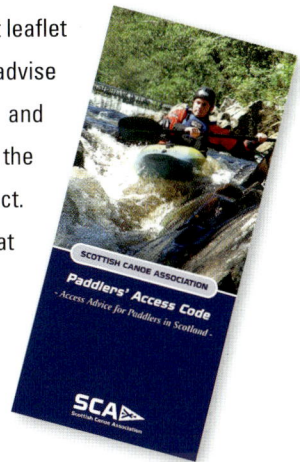

A small safe fire on a beach well away from woodland.
Photo | Donald Macpherson

Wildlife

As in the rest of the Highlands, the Great Glen is home to a rich variety of wildlife. From our largest mammal, the beautiful red deer to tiny bats, there is a great deal to discover. Here's some information on the main species of wildlife you might meet on your adventure. Pick up a wildlife viewing card from the Caledonian Canal offices at Corpach and Seaport Marina to report back on what you've seen. This helps to provide up-to-date information on wildlife populations.

On the land

Red squirrels

Is there a more beautiful woodland animal than the red squirrel? Despite their popularity, Scotland's red squirrels are one of our most threatened species. Without urgent help they could become extinct in Scotland before the end of this century.

Once found across Britain, red squirrels have disappeared from most of England and Wales. Scotland has the largest proportion of these animals and the Highlands are one of the few places where red squirrels exist in the absence of their main threat, the introduced North American grey. It is a more robust competitor and carries squirrel pox which is fatal to reds. Conservation efforts to keep the Highlands grey-free involve measures to prevent the spread of greys and management of conifer forests as red squirrel strongholds, unsuitable for greys if they do arrive.

Red deer

There is a good chance that you'll come across a native red deer along the trail. The majestic red deer is our largest land mammal, and undoubtedly one of the most impressive wildlife spectacles of Scotland; their sights and sounds are enjoyed by locals, visitors and 'Autumn Watch' viewers alike. They are found in woodland, on moorland and to the tops of mountains. They are widespread throughout

Red deer. Photo | Scottish Natural Heritage

Roe deer. Photo | Scottish Natural Heritage

the Highlands and live mostly on high ground, but venture further down in search of food when winter comes.

Roe deer

The striking and delicate roe deer is found throughout mainland Scotland, wherever there is a tiny patch of cover where they can hide by day.

Wild deer play an important part in our rural economy and culture, are an integral part of Scotland's biodiversity, and provide us with healthy food and recreational opportunities. Do keep a look out for them when driving on Highland roads at night.

Pine martens

The pine marten was once found throughout Britain but by the turn of the 20th century the once widespread distribution was confined to small populations in North West Scotland, where the species survived in areas of remote forest and rocky moorland. In 1988 the species was given full legal protection.

While the pine marten population is now increasingly widespread in Scotland, it is still rare in Britain. They are hard to catch a glimpse of as they spend most of their time in woodland and are mostly active at night. Well done if you spot one!

Wildcats

The distinctively marked and distinctly shy wildcat is one of the most elusive and enigmatic of our predators. It is certainly amongst our rarest, having been persecuted in Britain since the Middle Ages. The population probably reached its lowest level around 1914, when it was believed to be confined to the north and west of Scotland. Estimates of wildcat numbers in Scotland have varied between 1,000 and 4,000, but there may be fewer than 400 cats with classic wildcat markings surviving. They are a European Protected Species and therefore fully protected.

Pine marten. Photo | Scottish Natural Heritage

Wildcat. Photo | Scottish Natural Heritage

WILDLIFE

In the water

Dolphins and porpoises

The waters around Scotland are among the finest in Europe for seeing dolphins and porpoises. The Moray Firth at the end of the trail is home to the only known resident population of bottlenose dolphins in the North Sea. This is a small population of about 120 animals that ranges throughout the Moray Firth and all the way down the east coast at least as far as the Firth of Forth. The Moray Firth Special Area of Conservation was created to protect the bottlenose dolphins that use this important area. Dolphins are a European Protected Species.

Atlantic salmon

You'll find Atlantic salmon in the temperate waters of Lochaber. They live in freshwater as juveniles but migrate to sea as adults before returning to spawn. Atlantic salmon return to their native river, and even the same stretch of the river from which they were born, with amazing accuracy. This means that many different 'populations' of Atlantic salmon may exist within the same river.

Salmon spawn between November and December but in some larger rivers this may extend from October to late February. After spawning about 90–95% of all Atlantic salmon die. Some do, however, survive and some may spawn twice or more. Depending on the water temperature and the availability of food, young fish will live in the river for two to three years. Once they reach a size of around 12cm, they change to allow them to survive in marine environments. The young fish turn silver, and start to leave the rivers during the late spring. Most of these fish will be gone by June.

Brown trout

The brown trout is one of Scotland's most recognisable native fish and is found in rivers, large lochs and upland lochans. This species has two alternative life-cycles – the first is the freshwater resident form referred to as

79

Dolphin. Photo | Scottish Natural Heritage

Salmon. Photo | Scottish Natural Heritage

Otter. Photo | Scottish Natural Heritage

'brown trout' and the second is the sea-going form referred to as 'sea trout'.

'Resident' brown trout complete the whole of their life cycle in fresh water. Most populations do, however, undertake significant migrations within fresh water. The most common life-cycle pattern in Scottish brown trout populations is the migration of juvenile fish from nursery areas, where they begin to feed, into lochs where they may remain until becoming adults.

(See page 87 for more information on fishing in the Great Glen)

Otters

The otter, also known in North West Scotland by its Gaelic name *Dobhran* and *Beaste Dubh* (black beast), belongs to the same family as badgers, weasels, stoats, pine marten and mink. Scotland is a European stronghold for the otter. When pesticide pollution of waterways eliminated otters from most of England and Wales, they survived in Scotland's cleanest waterways in the north and west. Now the population has recovered, otters can be spotted in many areas, but particularly on the west coast and the islands. Otters are largely solitary, semi-aquatic mammals that obtain most of their food from lochs, rivers or the sea. The Scottish population is unusual in that it comprises a particularly high proportion (perhaps 50% or more) of coastal-dwelling individuals that feed almost exclusively in the sea.

In the air

Ospreys

After persecution in the early 20th century, Ospreys are now successfully re-establishing themselves in the west of Scotland and may be spotted all along the Great Glen during your trip. Watch out for the awe-inspiring sight of an osprey diving claws first into the water to catch its prey. These beautiful birds of prey don't live here all year long – they spend early summer here and return to Africa when the weather turns cooler in August/September.

Young ospreys in the nest.
Photo | Forestry Commission Picture Library / Neill Campbell

Herons

The grey heron found in this area and across the UK is the largest European heron. Keep an eye out along the way for the elegant grey heron by the riverside or overhead. These solitary birds stalk their prey, standing motionless by the waterside with neck outstretched for a long time as they wait for mealtime.

Heron. Photo | Peter Sandground Photography

Bats

There are at least nine species of these flying mammals in Scotland, of which the most numerous and familiar are pipistrelles, which can be seen flitting about near woodland or open water at dusk, in search of midges and other flying insects. Luckily for all of us, a single pipistrelle bat can eat up to 3,000 midges in one night!

You may also see buzzards, eagles, siskins and lesser spotted woodpeckers.

Daubenton's bat. Photo | Scottish Natural Heritage

Things to See and Do

Whether you fancy a rest day, want to explore the area or the weather has forced you off the water, you'll find lots of things to see and do in the Great Glen. Here are just a few ideas for those something-different days.

Around Fort William

Nevis Range

There's a huge range of outdoor activities throughout the year and for all abilities – gondola cable car, skiing and snowboarding, mountain biking, forest walks, family cycling, and the new high wire adventure course.

Torlundy, Fort William, PH33 6SQ

☏ 01397 705 825

www.nevisrange.co.uk

Ben Nevis Distillery

Join a guided tour and taste the whisky at one of Scotland's oldest distilleries.

Lochy Bridge, Fort William, PH33 6TJ

☏ 01397 700200

www.bennevisdistillery.com

Ben Nevis Visitor Centre

Find out about walks in Glen Nevis and the mountain track up Britain's highest mountain at 1,345m.

☏ 01349 781401

www.highlifehighland.com/bennevis/visitor-centre

Loch Lochy area

Eagle Barge Inn, Laggan

A converted Dutch barge, the Eagle is a unique restaurant and pub that floats in the Caledonian Canal.

Laggan Locks; South Laggan; Near Invergarry; PH34 4EA

☏ 07789 858567

www.eaglebargeinn.weebly.com

📷 *Caledonian Canal Visitor Centre. Photo | Scottish Canals*

Loch Oich area

Loch Oich Food Co.

Great coffee shop, and breakfast and brunch restaurant.

Well of Seven Heads, off A82, Nr Invergarry

📞 01809 501246

Bridge of Oich

An innovative suspension bridge built in 1845.

Near Aberchalder

NH 338 036

Fort Augustus area

Caledonian Canal Visitor Centre

Discover the stories and history of the amazing waterway you are travelling on.

Ardchattan House, Canalside, Fort Augustus, PH32 4BA

📞 01320 366493

Loch Ness area

Falls of Foyers

This short, spectacular walk takes you to one of the hidden gems of Loch Ness. Follow the waymarked paths to see the spectacular waterfall cascading down a gorge into the loch.

Near Foyers

Start of walk NH 498 205

Invermoriston Bridge

Built in 1813 by Thomas Telford, the engineer who was also responsible for the Caledonian Canal. The bridge was built to support the canal works and create a much improved road infrastructure. It is situated next to the new bridge which was built in 1930.

NH 419 165

📷 *Dores Inn. Photo | Donald Macpherson*

Urquhart Castle

Discover intriguing history and amazing views at this dramatic castle ruin on the shore of Loch Ness.

Inverness, IV63 6XJ

☎ 01456 450551

www.historic-scotland.gov.uk

Dores Inn

Set on the shore of Loch Ness, a family run restaurant and pub. To book a table please call the team at the Dores Inn. Open 7 days – all vintages welcome!

Dores, IV1 2TR

☎ 01463 751203

www.thedoresinn.co.uk

Some more ideas

Have a look at local visitor information websites for other inspiring things to do in the Great Glen.

www.visitscotland.com

www.outdoorcapital.co.uk

Other useful web links

www.greatglencanoetrail.info

www.greatglenway.com

www.scottishcanals.co.uk

www.forestry.gov.uk

www.outdooraccess-scotland.com

www.dolphinspace.org

www.marinecode.org

www.explorehighland.com

Activities

Cycling

How about paddling the Great Glen Trail and returning by bicycle? The Great Glen Way is a mountain bike route running 73 miles from Inverness to Fort William.

It's best to allow at least three days, four is even better. A mountain bike is essential as although a lot of the trail is on the towpath and there are some road sections, some of it is rough and hilly, rising to 300m. Travel light and consider staying in hostels or B&Bs.

It's possible to hire a bike in Inverness and leave it in Fort William. If you have your own bikes you can use a bicycle taxi service to get your bikes to the right end of the trail.

if you are in a hurry you could cycle the northern section of the Caledonia Way, part of the National Route 78. This 66 mile route between Inverness and Fort William avoids the rough sections of The Great Glen Way by using quiet roads on the south side of Lock Ness. It can be completed comfortably in two days or even one if you are really in a hurry. A mountain bike is not neccessary for this alternative. For a more off-road version try the South Loch Ness Trail.

For bike hire and taxi service:

Ticket to Ride, Inverness
www.tickettoridehighlands.co.uk
📞 01463 419160

Nevis Cycles, Fort William
www.neviscycles.com
📞 01397 705555

Great Glen Way
www.highland.gov.uk/greatglenway/

National Route 78
www.sustrans.org.uk

South Loch Ness Trail
https://www.visitinvernesslochness.com/explore-the-scottish-highlands/the-south-loch-ness-trail/

Fishing

What could be better than setting up camp after a day's paddling and cooking up a fish that you've just caught? This area is renowned for its fishing. The Caledonian Canal and its lochs (Loch Lochy, Loch Oich, Loch Ness and Loch Dochfour) are home to salmon and sea trout, pike, rainbow trout and brown trout. And if you've ventured off the canal you'll find good salmon fishing on the rivers too. The fishing season runs from March through to the end of September.

Catching your own dinner on the trail can certainly add to the adventure but before you 'sling your hook' there are some things you need to know. You cannot just fish anywhere in Scotland. Your rights under the Scottish Outdoor Access Code do not extend to fishing. Unlike in England and Wales, there is no national rod licence in Scotland and there are strict rules about what you can catch and where. If you'd like to try catching your own fish supper when you're on the Canoe Trail, you may need to get permission in advance and make sure you're aware of the rules – see www.outdooraccess-scotland.com for more details on what you can and can't do.

The law regarding migratory species including salmon and sea trout is very strict and covers the whole country. All anglers must have written permission to fish – usually issued by the land-owner or a club. You cannot fish for salmon or sea trout on a Sunday and you are not allowed to sell any of your catch.

The law is different for all other species of fish. You only need written permission if there is a Protection Order in place for the area you'd like to fish in. Find out more from the local contacts given below.

Bait, tackle and permits can be obtained from The Rod & Gun Shop, High Street, Fort William, PH33 6AT, ☎ 01397 702656. The shop also has a comprehensive contacts list on their website. This details who to contact for permission to fish on most of the rivers and lochs in the Great Glen. See www.fortwilliamfishing.com/index-files/page711.htm

At the other end of the trail, you can buy or hire fishing equipment and bait from Grahams of Inverness Ltd, 37/39 Castle Street, Inverness, IV2 3DU, ☎ 01463 233178. See www.grahamsonline.co.uk

📷 *Local fisherman on Loch Ness*
Photo | John Macpherson Photography

📷 *Homemade downwind sail in use on Loch Ness. Photo | John Macpherson Photography*

Canoe sailing

Canoe sailing is a great alternative to paddling open water. Using nature's energy to take you where hopefully you want to go not only gives the arms a great rest but is great fun too. Although canoe sailing is recognised as a discipline in itself you don't need expensive equipment to sail.

The conditions need to be just right for you to sail. Too light a breeze and you are probably better off paddling, too strong a wind and you might be better taking a rest onshore.

One of the simplest means of sailing down-wind is by using a bivi bag and a set of paddles. You have to be paddling tandem and carrying a spare paddle to do this. The bow paddler uses the two canoe poles inside the bivi bag to create a V–shaped sail, while the stern paddler controls the boat by using rudder/ steering strokes. Keep an eye out on what's happening around you – remember that the sail can block your view.

You can also buy downwind sails off the shelf and the latest styles include clear panels so that you can see through the sail and control your canoe safely. These sails generally have two sleeves at the top corners for the ends of canoe poles and releasable clips at the bottom to secure the sail onto the front of the canoe. Using canoe poles rather than paddles means the sail catches more wind and travels more briskly down the loch.

Another simple option is to create an A-frame mast using canoe poles when two or more canoes are rafted together. Depending on the size of your sail and the wind conditions, you can use either half or full length poles to

📷 *Commercially available downwind sails in action on Loch Ness. Photo | Donald Macpherson*

create a suitable sized A frame to support a larger spinnaker type sail or even a tarp as a sail sheet.

Experienced canoeists develop their own systems of sailing including using sailing thwarts, masts, foot mounts, leeboards, tarps to stabilise and strengthen the sail and even use specially designed sails.

For safety reasons you should be able to pull in the sail quickly if you have to stop or slow down for any reason.

When sailing downwind as a group, be aware that the group can spread out quite quickly. If there is an accident and someone in the group capsizes, you may find it difficult to paddle back upwind to help them.

In some instances the best option might be to raft canoes together to help create a more stable platform and the bow paddlers can then share a sail.

When sailing, always be aware of your surroundings and other waterway traffic. Canoe sail in clear areas and revert back to paddle power when in busy locations.

Loch Lochy and Loch Ness are ideal locations to canoe sail. Canoe sailing is not permitted on the Caledonian Canal sections of the trail.

Index

INDEX

KIDZ **ZIP** PFD

PEAK UK

www.peakuk.com

You won't believe a recycled jacket could feel this good

TEREK

Supple, soft and quiet, the three-layer breathable waterproof fabric of this jacket is made from 100% recycled nylon from post-industrial waste (Global Recycled Standard certificate CU818073). Tread lightly in the Terek jacket.

Palm

STOP
THE SPREAD

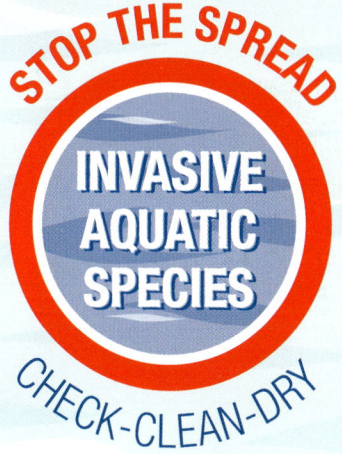

STOP THE SPREAD
INVASIVE AQUATIC SPECIES
CHECK-CLEAN-DRY

Are you unknowingly spreading invasive species on your water sports equipment and clothing?

Invasive species can affect fish and other wildlife, restrict navigation, clog up propellers and be costly to manage. You can help protect the water sports you love by following three simple steps when you leave the water.

CHECK — **Check** your equipment and clothing for live plants and animals - particularly in areas that are damp or hard to inspect.

CLEAN — **Clean** and wash all equipment, footwear and clothing thoroughly.

If you do come across any plants or animals, leave them at the water body where you found them.

DRY — **Dry** all equipment and clothing - some species can live for many days in moist conditions.

Make sure you don't transfer water elsewhere.

For more information go to www.nonnativespecies.org and click Check Clean Dry

Scottish Canals

THE GREEN BLUE
A joint BMF and RYA initiative

Scottish Natural Heritage
Dualchas Nàdair na h-Alba
All of nature for all of Scotland
Nàdar air fad airson Alba air fad

NNSS
GB non-native species secretariat

RAFTS

SCA
Scottish Canoe Association

SEPA
Scottish Environment
Protection Agency

natural scotland
SCOTTISH GOVERNMENT

EXPLORE HIGHLAND

by Canoe... by Kayak... by SUP...

Full outfitting & support service for the Canoe Trail

Canoe, Kayak & Paddleboard Guided Trips
Private Group Bookings
Interactive Guide Map
Emergency Uplifts
Canoe Hire

EXPLORE HIGHLAND
Unit 4B, 23 Harbour Road,
Inverness, IV1 1SY.
info@explorehighland.com
www.explorehighland.com